THE ISRAELIS
HOW THEY LIVE AND WORK

40p

The Israelis

HOW THEY LIVE AND WORK

Brian Dicks

DAVID & CHARLES
NEWTON ABBOT
LONDON

For Marion and Gerald

ISBN 0 7153 7035 9

© Brian Dicks 1975

Photoset and printed
in Great Britain by
REDWOOD BURN LIMITED
Trowbridge & Esher
for David & Charles (Holdings) Limited
South Devon House Newton Abbot Devon

Contents

INTRODUCTORY NOTE   ix

1 THE JEWS, PALESTINE AND ISRAEL   1
The beginnings . return to Palestine . the Diaspora . occupation and dispersal . Ottoman rule . the Zionist Movement . the Balfour Declaration . the partition plans . the State of Israel

2 THE COUNTRY AND THE PEOPLE   19
Geography . climate . flora and fauna . population and immigration . the Jewish population . language . the non-Jewish population . urban Israel . Tel Aviv . Jerusalem . Haifa . rural settlement

3 HOW THE COUNTRY IS RUN   43
President and constitution . the Knesset and cabinet . the electoral system . political parties . national institutions . justice and the legal system . local government . the civil service . police and prisons . national defence . currency and finance

4 HOW THEY LIVE   60
Housing . national insurance . social welfare . health services . maternal and child welfare . food and drink

5 HOW THEY WORK   76
Agriculture . irrigation and conservation . principal agricultural products . fruit crops . industrial crops . other crops . livestock and dairy produce . forestry . fisheries . energy and natural resources . manufacturing industry . the tourist industry . labour and working conditions . trade unionism . wages and income tax

509599

6 HOW THEY GET ABOUT   99
   Development of the road system . modern road improvements . traffic and public transport . rail . air .
   domestic air travel . shipping . ports . Haifa . Ashdod .
   Eilat

7 HOW THEY LEARN   114
   Development of Jewish education . the multi-trend system .
   state education . primary schooling . educational and cultural differences . secondary education . orthodox schools .
   Arab education . *kibbutz* education . adult education . higher
   education . research institutes

8 HOW THEY AMUSE THEMSELVES   131
   Festivals and holidays . outdoor and sporting activities . cultural pursuits . the press . radio and television . cinema .
   theatre . music . art . literature

9 HINTS FOR VISITORS   147

   BIBLIOGRAPHY   151
   ACKNOWLEDGEMENTS   152
   INDEX   153

List of Illustrations

View of Jerusalem from the Mount of Olives   37
Central Tel Aviv from the Shalom Tower   37
The Negev, Israel's toughest challenge   38
Horticulture at Ein Gedi *kibbutz*, Dead Sea (*Israel Government Tourist Office*)   38
The Moslem quarter, Old City, Jerusalem   55
The Mea Shearim district of West Jerusalem   55
Tomb of the Patriarchs, Hebron   56
The Shalom Tower, Tel Aviv   56
Housing estate, Jerusalem   73
Apartments under construction, Jerusalem   73
Vineyard of Ashdot Yaacob *kibbutz*, Galilee (*Israel Government Tourist Office*)   74
The Gibor tights factory (*Israel Government Tourist Office*)   74
The Carmel Market, Tel Aviv   91
Dizengoff Street, Tel Aviv   91
A first-aid lesson for elementary school children (*Israel Government Tourist Office*)   92
Railway station, Tel Aviv (*Israel Government Tourist Office*)   92

IN TEXT
The state of Israel and its neighbours   viii
Partition proposals and the growth of Israel   13
Israel: physical regions   20
Towns in Israel   32
Water projects   81
Communications infrastructure   102
Unless otherwise acknowledged the photographs are from the author's collection.

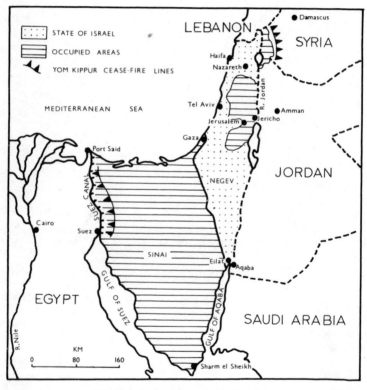

The State of Israel and its neighbours

Introductory Note

This book, in keeping with its companions in the series, is an attempt to convey to the reader the main characteristics and problems current in contemporary Israeli life. This aim alone has made its writing difficult, for it is not easy to approach the subject of Israel with indifference or, at best, cool objectivity. The mere existence of the state is a matter of controversy and the problems it faces are charged with emotional responses of extreme diversity. In part this is due to the fact that the country contains the shrines and Holy Places of three monotheistic religions and their incorporation within one political entity has never been universally accepted, not least by some Jewish factions within Israel's own borders.

As a political expression, Israel came into being with the declaration of its own independence on 14 May, 1948. The boundaries of the state were never defined by international agreement although its sovereignty was endorsed by the majority of world powers. But Israel was not recognised by the neighbouring Arab countries whose armies invaded the state on the very day independence was declared. Known to Israel as the War of Independence, this was the first major confrontation in the Arab—Israeli conflict which has provided the world with one of the most intractable and dangerous political problems. To the Arabs, the establishment of Israel by force was deeply humiliating and the desire for revenge has been the strongest unifying principle among the Arab states. Following the 1949 armistice agreements signed with Egypt, Syria, Jordan and Lebanon, Israel acquired a territory of approximately 20,700 square kilometres (7,900 square miles) that is, an area roughly equivalent to the size of Wales or the State of New Jersey. This territory was less extensive than the Palestine of the British mandate, but larger by about one-quarter than the area allocated to the Jews by the 1947 United Nations Special Committee on Palestine. In the north, north-east and west, Israel's boundaries with Lebanon, Syria and the natural frontier of the Mediterranean, respectively, were largely coincidental with those of mandated Palestine. In the south also, apart from the Gaza Strip, the frontier followed the old international boundary from the north-east corner of Egypt's Sinai peninsula south-eastwards to Eilat on the Gulf of Aqaba. To the east, however, the frontier with Jordan was complex and was created with the annexation by that country of the West Bank in 1949. This represented the 23 per cent of Palestine which remained in Arab hands. Until 1967, this eastern boundary ran through Jerusalem and divided the Jordanian-held Old City from West or New Jerusalem, the Israeli capital.

These provisionally fixed boundaries gave Israel a territorial length of 420 kilometres from the Lebanese border to Eilat in the south. The country's width, however, made it strategically vulnerable for it varied from only 10 kilometres at Eilat and 19 kilometres north of Tel Aviv to a maximum of 113 kilometres in the vicinity of Beersheba, where the triangular area of the Negev, bordering on Jordan and Egyptian Sinai, formed roughly 60 per cent of the country's land area. A particularly vulnerable region was the narrow neck of land to the north of Lake Kinneret, sandwiched between the Syrian Golan Heights and Lebanon. In June 1967, the Arab states again massed their troops along Israel's land borders and threatened a renewed war of annihilation. Israel, in what became known as the Six Day War, was successful in conquering not only the remaining territory of the former mandate—that is, Judaea, Samaria and East Jerusalem—but also Sinai, the Gaza Strip and the Golan Heights. These areas, covering an additional 68,659 square kilometres (26,500 square miles) of territory, were placed under military administration and, although precariously governed by cease-fire agreements, they transformed Israel into a much more viable strategic and political unit.

Israel's administration of these areas, and indeed the existence of the state itself, was challenged by the Yom Kippur War of October 1973. New cease-fire lines were agreed with Egypt and Syria, but the status of the administered territories has not changed since 1967. Pending a peace settlement, which will determine the political future of these areas, Israel's policy is one of maintaining security for Jews and Arabs alike and of encouraging coexistence and co-operation between the two peoples—perhaps as an optimistic model for the wider relationships between the state and the Arab countries.

In the following pages only passing reference is made to the problems and life styles of the administered areas for, with the exception of East Jerusalem, Israel has not annexed its conquests. The main body of this book deals with Israel as defined by the 1949 armistice agreements and, by and large, all statistics refer to this area. In this connection, however, it should be stressed that Israel, perhaps more than any other country, is in a rapid process of transition and what is written today becomes radically altered tomorrow. Changes occur at a bewildering rate in almost every sphere of national life and basic facts must be carefully adjusted.

1

The Jews, Palestine and Israel

THAT 'the past is the key to the present' is a much quoted maxim to introduce a discourse on history. In the case of the Jews and the establishment of Israel it is a particularly pertinent and valuable statement, for although the practical conception of an independent Jewish state, and the struggle to realise it, emerged only with the Zionist movement in the nineteenth century, it is impossible to understand the events since this time unless viewed against the background of early Jewish history. Problems concerning the country's internal solidarity, where the population consists of often incompatible elements, is primarily a function of the past, as is the cultural and idealistic gap between the older generations of Jews born in exile and the younger generations native to Israel. Similarly the Arab-Israeli conflict, which permeates every aspect of national life, must be seen in its historical context, for it is basically a conflict of religious ideals and nationalistic aspirations rather than one based on racial differences between Jew and Arab.

As a state, Israel is barely twenty-seven years old, but the unique attachment of the Jewish people to Palestine stretches back nearly 4,000 years to the era of the biblical Patriarchs. Although they were the ruling people of the country for only brief periods before the Romans destroyed the Temple and the city of Jerusalem, the generations of Jews in dispersal throughout the world continued to regard the land promised to their ancestors in antiquity as their spiritual home. Positive efforts were made to resettle Jews whenever foreign rule allowed and the continuity of Jewish urban and rural life was never completely broken. Following their expulsion from Spain and Portugal in the fifteenth century a remnant settled in Palestine,

1

of the Ottoman Empire, and during the 400 years of
(1517–1917), the Jews were a continuous and definite
in the population. It was a fundamental part of the
religious faith that they would return to their homeland
and these hopes and aspirations finally realised political form
with the establishment of a national centre in Palestine in 1948.

THE BEGINNINGS

Since antiquity, geographical position has been the dominant factor in the history of Palestine. Lying at the crossroads of
Asia, Africa and Europe, and exposed to the influences of the
Mediterranean Sea, Palestine was destined to be the disputed
prize of conquerors, tossed like a ball from empire to empire.
The Bible records the major events of this early history and,
increasingly, archaeological evidence has substantiated the
ancient traditions of this complex document. The Old Testament also emphasises another fundamental factor in history—the position of Palestine on the border between the desert
and the sown, and the unending struggle between the pastoral
and agricultural way of life. The Cain and Abel story reflects
the enmity which continued as a permanent element in the
local situation.

For the Jews, Palestine's real history begins with the migration from the east of pastoral Semitic tribes. One of the first of
these peoples, typical of the recurrent eruptions of nomads into
settled areas, is described in the biblical story of the patriar-
chal figure Abraham, the traditional founder of the Israelite
line. The people came from Ur in the Chaldees in Mesopotamia and probably included the ancestors of both Jewish and
Arab peoples, the former confining themselves to Palestine and
the latter penetrating farther south and joining with other
nomadic tribes in Arabia. The Old Testament is full of refer-
ences to peoples whose beginnings are similarly traced to a
single founder, but to the Jews such an idea was reinforced by a
belief that they were the chosen people, thereby emphasising
the purity of their descent from a patriarch singled out, especially, by God. The biblical account of the testing of Abraham

embodies the traditional covenant between God and man and the promise that Abraham's descendants would become a great nation.

The historicity of the Abraham tradition is now generally accepted by most scholars and, although there is difficulty in precisely dating the migration, the twentieth and nineteenth centuries BC have received most support. During the middle of the second millennium BC, when the leadership of the Abrahamites had passed to Isaac and then to Jacob, a series of droughts and crop failures led them to follow the example of other nomads and seek permission to pasture their flocks on the eastern fringes of the Nile estuary. The stories found in Exodus relate how they were persecuted and reduced to a state of servitude in the province of Goshen until they were led in revolt by a national figure, Moses. The time in Egypt and the Exodus are thought to have occurred between 1400 and 1200 BC. The effect made a profound impression on the Jews, one which was never forgotten in their subsequent history, and celebrated each year in the Festival of the Passover.

Return to Palestine

Under the leadership of Moses, the Jews returned to Palestine, though not before extensive tribal reorganisation was undertaken in the Sinai peninsula. Of vital importance to their religious and national future was the Mosaic Law which was later elaborated into a codification touching on every aspect of man's religious, social and economic behaviour—an ethical monotheism which was to form the bond of union with Christianity and Islam. The protracted conquest of Canaan was led by Joshua and the most spectacular battle was undoubtedly that of Jericho. The land was divided among twelve tribes, but this loose federation was unable to oppose effectively the organised armies of the Philistines, a people of Greek origin who had founded a chain of powerful city states along the southern coast at Gaza, Ashkelon, Ashdod, Ekron and Gat. The period of the Judges was one of tribal disunity and conflict with neighbouring foes, but leaders such as Gideon, Deborah and Samson emerged in times of national and military crises.

A new unified military power developed around 1025 BC when Saul was anointed king by Samuel. This succeeded in turning back the Philistine advance and Saul's successor, David (1010–970 BC), remained the ideal of a Hebrew king for all subsequent history and a prototype of the expected Messiah. David consolidated a large kingdom which extended into present-day Syria and Jordan, and his selection of Jerusalem as the Hebrew capital provided a strong strategic fortress and a major centre for the unity of the northern and southern tribes. Jerusalem's position as a religious centre had its beginnings when the Ark of the Covenant was brought to the city, an embodiment of the whole conception of the relationship between God, land and people. The period of greatness reached its zenith under David's son, Solomon (970–930 BC). The mineral resources of the country were tapped, trading and diplomatic treaties were made with neighbouring states, and the First Temple was built in Jerusalem.

The Diaspora

Decline set in with Solomon's death, and the Second Book of Kings describes the internal wars and the rapid succession of rulers. The former united state was divided into separate and often conflicting kingdoms, one centred on Samaria and preserving the name Israel, the other focussed on Jerusalem and known as the Kingdom of Judah. Dissension tempered the imperial ambitions of neighbouring states and after 720 BC Assyria incorporated the northern kingdom, and many of its inhabitants were deported. The Kingdom of Judah maintained its independence for more than a century longer, but finally fell to Nebuchadnezzar whose Babylonian Empire had become the greatest power of the region. Jerusalem was destroyed and the deportation to Babylon of a large portion of the population marked the first permanent and major division of the Jews after they had achieved a fully developed national consciousness. The Diaspora may be said to have begun in Babylon for a strong Jewish colony remained in Mesopotamia down to modern times.

Babylon fell to the Persians in 539 BC and, under Cyrus, the

Jews were allowed to return to Palestine to rebuild their Temple. According to Josephus only 42,000 elected to return, but the rebuilding, recorded in the Books of Ezra and Nehemiah, marked a period of Jewish cultural and religious revival. It is believed that the Mosaic Law, or Torah, took on its final form during this period and great works of teaching and devotion were written.

In 333 BC the Persian Empire collapsed under the advance of Alexander the Great and although the conqueror left the Jews very much to themselves the Hellenistic period was responsible for further Jewish emigration. Jews were among the first settlers in the new city of Alexandria, and other large colonies were established in Antioch and Rome, with smaller settlements in Cyprus, Crete, Asia Minor and around the Black Sea. The Jewish colonies adopted the Greek language, but maintained their own worship, and the synagogue, a new feature developed among Jews parted from Palestine and the Temple, served as a focus for religious life.

Many of the successors to Alexander's empire, especially the Seleucid rulers of Syria who incorporated Palestine in 198 BC, attempted to root out the Jewish faith and customs. The initial passive resistance among the Jews finally led to revolution, championed by Judas Maccabeaus. The Temple in Jerusalem was re-dedicated and Syria granted Judaea a measure of political autonomy. The remarkable Maccabean dynasty expanded the state to an area similar to that governed by David and Solomon. As such it remained until 63 BC when Roman legions under Pompei captured Jerusalem.

OCCUPATION AND DISPERSAL

The Roman occupation of Palestine marked the beginning of a long period of foreign control which was not lifted until after World War II. Rome found it exceedingly difficult to 'conquer' the ancient kingdom of the Jews and its rule was brutal and oppressive. Parts of Palestine were annexed to adjacent provinces but most of the area was declared a Roman Protectorate, which after 40 BC was 'ruled' by the House of

Herod in complete subservience to Rome. The ambitious construction projects of Herod the Great (37–34 BC) were attempts to appease the population for a cruel and inhumane government. He built a new Temple and many public buildings in Jerusalem, fortified the city, and rebuilt Samaria and other centres. The culmination of his building activity was the creation of the town and harbour of Caesarea which became the third largest port in the Mediterranean and, subsequently, the largest town and capital of Roman Palestine. Herod also built the royal fortress at Herodian, east of Bethlehem, and the desert retreat at Masada near the Dead Sea; the former was planned as a royal tomb and the latter as an impregnable fortress.

The Herodians were appointed and dismissed at the whims of the Roman emperors and direct Roman rule was often reimposed. A century of constant strife during which Messianic ferment was high and a new religion, Christianity, was born, culminated in the Jewish revolt of AD 66. After years of bitter fighting the uprising was suppressed in AD 70 when Jerusalem was taken by Titus and the Temple was destroyed. Jewish rebellion again broke out in AD 115 and in AD 132. The latter revolt, under the spiritual leadership of Rabbi Akiva and the military direction of Bar Kochba, lasted three years, when it was quelled by Hadrian and Jerusalem was destroyed. The city was rebuilt under the name of Aelia Capitolina, but Hadrian excluded the Jews from its walls. This move, together with the destruction of the Temple, were crushing blows to Jewish nationalism and, in spite of continuing intellectual leadership from within Palestine, the Jewish community became a dying branch. The rise of Christianity was also detrimental to the Jewish cause and when, under Constantine (AD 306–37), it was adopted as the state religion repressive legislation was introduced against Judaism. Palestine now became a favoured region as the place of origin of Christianity and the spiritual centre of Judaism was transferred to Persia where the Jews enjoyed religious tolerance.

Ottoman rule

A decisive chapter to the history of Palestine was added in the seventh century when it was conquered by the Arabs and incorporated into the vast Moslem Empire. The new religion, Islam, was a product of Judaism, and Jerusalem, along with Mecca and Medina, became a major Islamic 'Holy Place'. Between the eleventh and thirteenth centuries, the Christian rulers of Europe launched a series of Crusades against the 'infidel', believing they were re-establishing the Kingdom of Jerusalem. The precarious hold on the country was broken in 1291 when the loss of Acre returned Palestine to Moslem rule under the Egyptian Mameluke dynasty. In 1517, Egypt and Syria were conquered by the Ottoman Turks and Palestine was ruled for 400 years by feudal chieftains owing allegiance to the sultans of Constantinople.

Throughout the Ottoman period Palestine had no political or administrative significance and was a vague, undefined, expression for the southern part of the Turkish province of Syria. The Jews, however, driven out from the Diaspora countries, were again becoming a formative element in the population. They gravitated mainly to the four Holy Cities—Jerusalem, Hebron, Safad and Tiberius—and in Jerusalem, after 1872, Jews formed a majority over the combined Moslem and Christian populations. This Jewish settlement, known as the Old Yishuv, was largely parasitic and consisted of students and scholars of religion and those who had returned to end their days in Zion. They existed largely on charity from Jewish communities overseas and evinced neither marked political attitudes nor significant economic activity. Their settlement, however, had ushered in an important period of Jewish learning and their very presence in Palestine offered a significant base and encouragement for subsequent Zionist activity.

THE ZIONIST MOVEMENT

The survival of the Jews in the Diaspora rested on their sense of ethnic, religious and cultural identity and on their unique attachment, if often symbolic and romantic, to the land of Israel. In the eighteenth and nineteenth centuries the Jews shared in the general emancipation and economic expansion of Western Europe, and liberalism and assimilation appeared to be steadily gaining ground. In Russia and Eastern Europe, however, where the concentration of Jewish population was greatest, persecution and anti-semitism reached grave proportions. For the Jewish communities, the effect was to transform romantic nationalism into solid political ideals based on the re-creation of a Jewish homeland in Palestine. The conversion of the first nationalistic stirrings of Zionism into a dramatic international movement was the work of Theodor Herzl, an Austrian Jew and man of letters. In 1897, the first Zionist Congress at Basle adopted a resolution favouring 'a home in Palestine' for the Jews. In view of the distress of the Jews fleeing from Eastern Europe, it is interesting to note that Herzl was prepared to accept from Joseph Chamberlain, Britain's Colonial Secretary, a Jewish National Home in British East Africa. This is generally referred to as the 'Uganda Offer', though the area in question was in Kenya. The East Africa project was defeated in 1902, partly through the impassioned opposition of other Zionist leaders who could envisage no national home other than Palestine, and partly because there was already a steady flow of Jews to Palestine from Eastern Europe.

In Zionist annals this early Jewish immigration is known as the First Aliyah (literally 'going up') and the newcomers, together with the pietists of the Old Yishuv, provided a crucial opening wedge for further Jewish expansion. The attainment of economic goals was not the prime objective of these settlers, rather they hoped to find in Palestine a last bastion of traditionalism and they regarded land settlement ('the return to the soil') as a primary condition for the rejuvenation of the Jewish people. The First Aliyah wave (1882–1903) brought 20–30,000 immigrants to Palestine and agricultural settlements, such as Petah Tikvah, Rishon Le Zion, Hadera, Zikhron Yaakov and Rosh Pina, together with others in the Wilderness of Zin in the Negev, were established in the midst of an Ottoman-controlled region. At this early stage the relationship between the Jewish communities and the Arab population was largely characterised by mutual indifference. Their European background, literacy, social structure and agricultural methods, however, clearly differentiated the Jews from the mass of Arab peasantry, but friction arose only when Jews violated customary Arab rights of watering and pasturage.

The major objective of Zionism, to establish a viable Jewish enclave in Palestine, encountered strong opposition from the Jews themselves. Many feared that Zionism would jeopardise the position of flourishing Jewish communities in other parts of the world, more especially in the Middle East. Others, the ultra-orthodox Jews, objected to the political aspect of the movement, believing that the return to Zion could only be brought about by divine intervention and not by temporal agencies. But Zionism's major opponents came from outside Jewry and Herzl's consistent pleas for a settlement charter for Palestine gained little support amongst the major powers. Following his death in 1904, the Zionists turned to fostering a more intensive practical settlement in Palestine. Land acquisition was financed by the Jewish National Fund and the Palestine Foundation Fund, and Zionism spread throughout the world as a quasi-political movement with leftist, rightist and centre factions.

Herzl had denounced illegal infiltration as fruitless and self-defeating to the original aims of Zionism. The year 1904, however, marked the beginnings of a new wave of immigration, the Second Aliyah, which continued until the outbreak of World War I. During this period, 35–40,000 Jews entered Palestine, mainly from Russia, where the October Revolution of 1905 had ended in pogroms. The majority of these immigrants enjoyed a good education and many had technical training in agriculture. More important, however, they came with fixed socialist ideas and an ideology, of sorts, fashioned by the Russian revolution in which they had taken an active part. The majority were opposed to hired labour and private ownership of property, and were themselves ready to provide for their settlements the security which the Turkish authorities were reluctant to give. Degania in Galilee (founded in 1909) has the distinction of being the first collective settlement in Palestine, but by 1914, when the Jewish population had risen to around 80,000, there were 12,000 working the land in similarly organised collective farming communities.

The Second Aliyah is considered as a workers' or labour immigration in which the initiative and energy of the newcomers changed the whole structure of the Jewish population and laid the foundations of the labour movement in Palestine. In addition, the period witnessed the commencement of the World Zionist Organisation in Palestine (1908) and the beginnings of Jewish urban development, for in 1909 the foundations of Tel Aviv, the all-Jewish town were laid. To the Turks, however, the Jews were merely a source for taxation and they lacked juridicial status. This precarious situation is illustrated by the developments of December 1914 when the Turkish governor of Jaffa ordered the 6,000 Jews living in the port city to be expelled from the country. This edict led the Jewish communal leaders to urge all Jews domiciled in Palestine to apply for Ottoman citizenship and within weeks an effective naturalisation campaign had avoided the dangers of mass expulsion. But in 1915 a systematic Ottoman attack was launched on the entire Jewish redemptive effort and equally harsh measures were directed against renascent Arab nationalism which was active in attacking Ottoman misrule and decadence.

During World War I the centre of gravity of the World Zionist Organisation was transported to Britain where Chaim Weizmann occupied a position comparable to that held by Herzl in Central Europe up to 1904. Born in Motol in White Russia in 1874, Weizmann settled in Britain in 1902, a country he regarded as having a genuine sympathy for the Jewish cause. Professionally he was a distinguished chemist and became attached to Manchester University in 1906. His time was divided between academic studies and Zionist ideals, and his personal contacts with British political leaders as the result of both interests bore fruit in an Anglo-Zionist Alliance. Weizmann's notable contribution to the British war effort was the development of an improved process for the manufacture of acetone, the solvent used in the production of the naval explosive, cordite. This earned him the gratitude of Lloyd George, but this statesman's support of Zionism was essentially political, in the hope that it would bolster British postwar interests in the Middle East and have immediate wartime propaganda value.

The Balfour Declaration

In November 1917 the Balfour Declaration pledged the British government to 'use their best endeavours to the establishment in Palestine of a national home for the Jewish people'. The document, endorsed by France and Italy, was also approved by the United States, and when written into the League of Nations Mandate for Palestine it supplied the political and legal basis for Jewish efforts to redeem the homeland—the equivalent of the charter for which Herzl had struggled. The declaration, however, also made clear that nothing would be done to 'prejudice' the civil and religious rights of the non-Jewish communities (that is, the Arabs), to which a number of vague promises had already been made by Britain. Hussein, head of the Hashemite family of the Hejaz, was among those of the earlier Arab nationalists who aspired to leadership. In 1915, he corresponded with Sir Henry McMahon, British High Commissioner in Egypt, to discuss conditions on which the Arabs would rebel against the Turks. The rising would be concerted with a British drive from Egypt to push back the Turks from the eastern bank of the Suez Canal. Hussein's support was as much a function of clan rivalry as disillusionment with Turkish policy, and his objective was an Arab empire, embracing all the Arabic-speaking peoples, Moslem and Christian, and one independent of foreign influence and control. In the McMahon documents he claimed an area fronted by the Mediterranean in the west, Iran in the east and a line drawn through south-east Anatolia in the north. In December 1917 General Allenby entered Jerusalem and the 400 years of Turkish rule came to an end. By 1918, the whole of the Levant had been conquered and fell under a British military administration until July 1920 when Palestine, like Iraq, was made a mandated territory under British colonial administration.

It was natural that the Jewish world interpreted the Balfour Declaration as a major move towards the establishment of Zionist ideals, especially when, in 1918, Britain sent a Zionist Commission to Palestine with Weizmann as one of the representatives of Anglo-Jewry. The Third Jewish Aliyah had begun when World War I was still raging and between 1919 and 1923 a further 35,000 immigrants entered Palestine. They consisted, in the main, of young people who had trained through pioneer organisations prior to departure and who were willing to do any work the country might require of them. Initially, the Arab leaders were not opposed to Jewish immigration or to the establishment of a Zionist state, and in 1919 the Emir Faisal, leader of the Arab forces and later ruler of Iraq, signed an agreement with Weizmann pledging co-operation between Jews and Arabs, providing that an Arab state was set up in surrounding territories. Early in 1921 Winston Churchill, in an effort to cement Britain's relationship with the Arabs, detached the territory east of the Jordan and Abdullah was appointed emir of the newly created Transjordan.

THE PARTITION PLANS

The structure of the mandatory government followed the familiar British colonial pattern with a high commissioner exercising wide authority and assisted by a small all-British executive council of senior officials. The British garrison was commanded by an army and an air force officer responsible primarily to the War Office or the Air Ministry in London. Britain attempted little economic development, but it did provide an infrastructure for economic advancement. A modern system of civil administration was established, the country was mapped, road and railway communications were improved, and a modern deep water port was constructed at Haifa, followed by an oil refinery. The ports of Acre and Jaffa were also improved and a new roadstead was constructed at Tel Aviv.

Immigration provided the lever for economic development and during the Fourth Aliyah the Jewish population doubled on two occasions in the space of five years: from 84,000 to 150,000 in 1922–7 and from 175,000 to 384,000 in 1931–6. Both were periods of severe crisis for Jewish communities in Europe, the first bringing immigrants mainly from Poland and the second Jews from Germany. The unprecedented surge of immigration, however, led to a change of heart among the

Arab leaders and a more militant anti-Zionist nationalism emerged in Palestine. The intensity of Arab opposition grew

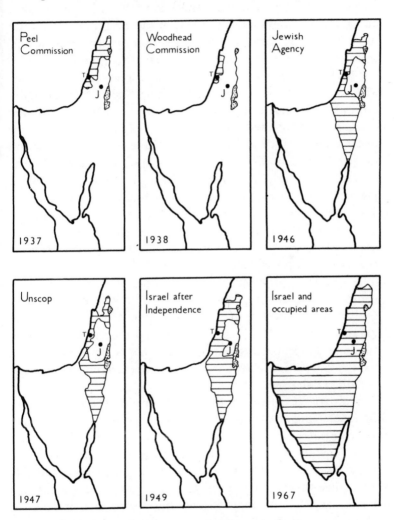

PARTITION PROPOSALS AND THE GROWTH OF ISRAEL
T – TEL AVIV　　　J – JERUSALEM

from the organised violence in 1929 to a war-like terror campaign in 1936–9. It now became clear that Jews and Arabs would not form a unified community and Britain found herself in an equivocal position, for promises had been made to both sides. In July 1939 a Royal Commission under Lord Peel's chairmanship advocated partition. The proposal was for a Jewish state to be set up in northern Palestine, the coastal plain and interior valleys, with the rest of the area attached to the Arab emirate of Transjordan, but with an outlet to the Mediterranean at Jaffa. Jerusalem was to remain a mandated state.

The Jewish response to this first partition plan was ambivalent, and the Arab response hostile. The Arabs objected on the grounds that partition would not only perpetuate a Zionist entity in Palestine, but would actually violate the territorial integrity of Palestine itself. Lord Samuel, the eminent Zionist and former high commissioner, opposed the plan partly for the reason that even in the proposed areas allocated to the Jewish state, Arabs would constitute nearly half the population. In 1938 the Woodhead Commission allocated an even smaller area to the Jews and this proposal was even less acceptable to the Zionists. Britain's answer was a policy aimed at stricter regulation of Jewish land purchase and immigration in the hope that such prohibition would ultimately lead to the establishment of an independent unitary state in whose government both peoples would co-operate. Throughout World War II illegal refugees from Nazi Europe were deported to Cyprus, Mauritius, and even back to Europe, and this policy, especially in view of German atrocities to Jews, led to extremist Zionist terrorism in Palestine.

The deportation policy was continued after the war and anti-British feeling among Jews was intensive. In 1945–6 a further plan for partition was proposed by both British and American governments. This was rejected by the Arabs as it failed to make Palestine a unified state, and by the Jews since it failed to guarantee their control of immigration and land transfer. In February 1947 Britain referred the entire question to the United Nations and its Special Committee on Palestine recommended that the mandate should end and the country be divided into Jewish and Arab areas. The Jewish state was to include much of northern Palestine, except for a pocket of land fronting the Lebanese border, together with the coastal lowlands from south of Tel Aviv to Haifa, and the Negev with the port of Eilat on the Gulf of Aqaba. The Arabs were to receive the central and eastern area including Nablus, Jerusalem, Bethlehem and Hebron, and the strip of Mediterranean coast from Gaza to the Egyptian border. In accordance with the United Nations resolution, the British terminated the mandate and the Jews, who accepted the proposals, proceeded with arrangements for the transitional move to independence. On 14 May 1948 a National Council, set up in Tel Aviv to establish a government, proclaimed the establishment of the State of Israel. The government was headed by David Ben-Gurion, the former chairman of the Jewish Agency Executive in Jerusalem, and Chaim Weizmann, the veteran Zionist leader, became the country's first president. As part of the Proclamation of Independence, Israel was declared 'open to Jewish immigration and to the ingathering of exiles'.

THE STATE OF ISRAEL

The United Nations resolution on partition brought to a head the barely concealed civil war in Palestine. Arab hostility to the establishment of any kind of Jewish state had led to a military offensive against the Jews long before the end of the mandate. The brunt of the Jewish offensive fell on the Haganah, an underground citizen army sponsored by organisations such as the Labour Federation and the Jewish Agency. The work of the Haganah, however, was complicated by the coexistence of other smaller organisations which, in effect, were terrorist, and whose irresponsibility damaged rather than promoted the Jewish cause. The destruction of a wing of Jerusalem's King David Hotel, was one of their violently 'patriotic' reprisals.

On the day the partition resolution was approved in New York, the first Arab attack was made on Jerusalem, and within hours of independence Arab armies from Egypt, Jordan and Iraq, with smaller forces from Syria and Lebanon, moved into Israel from all sides. Outnumbered and with few heavy weapons, the odds were heavily against Israel's survival, but the country was fighting for its very existence and the Arab armies were badly organised, so that the Jews were able to push them back on almost every front. The war, interspersed with truces and ceasefires, terminated on 29 December 1948, and Israel emerged with much more territory than that originally allocated under the partition plan. The Old City of Jerusalem, the Nablus and Hebron hills (Samaria and Judaea) and the middle Jordan valley remained in Arab hands and were added to Jordan, and the Gaza Strip went to Egypt. Armistice agreements were negotiated in a series of bilateral meetings between Israel and the Arab states, but these agreements failed to develop into a peace treaty.

A tragic consequence of the war was the plight of nearly a million Palestinian Arab refugees who moved into Syria, Lebanon, Jordan and the Gaza strip. The mass exodus was partly due to the fear of Jewish reprisals and partly the result of the insistence of Arab leaders to evacuate probable battle areas. The problem of the refugees, intensified by the 1967 June War, has raised bitter controversy around the world and has added fuel to the fire of discontent between Arab and Jew. The refugee camps became the breeding grounds for terrorism and the centres for anti-Jewish reprisals.

In December 1949 a Conciliation Committee was set up by the Security Council of the United Nations to negotiate a peace treaty. Hopes for a quick political settlement, however, were quashed through the Arab refusal to meet Israel at the Lausanne conference. From 1953 onwards tension became more and more acute, border incidents multiplied, and a series of *fedayin* (commando) raids, deep into Israeli territory, murdered civilians, destroyed installations and disrupted communications. The purchase by Egypt, in 1955, of Soviet-bloc armament and aircraft was countered by Israel obtaining jet aircraft and weapons from France, despite the fact that in May 1950 France, Britain and the United States had signed a declaration to prevent an arms race in the Middle East. Israel's position was further jeopardised by Nasser's military build-up in Sinai and the blockade in the Suez Canal and Gulf of Aqaba of Israeli vessels and any ships carrying cargo to or from Israel. In 1956 the balance of power was restored in Israel's favour when the Egyptian bases were wiped out and Israeli forces reached the Suez Canal and cleared the Gulf of Aqaba. In spite of strong

United Nations disapproval, Israel deferred the withdrawal of its troops from Egyptian territory until UN emergency forces had been stationed in the Gaza Strip and along the Straits of Tiran at the entrance to the Gulf of Aqaba. The latter made possible the development of the port of Eilat and fostered trading relations between Israel and East African and Asian countries.

The following decade was a period of relative 'peace' between Arab and Israeli forces. Egypt and Syria, however, with the aid of Soviet capital, weapons and training, were steadily developing their armies and defences. In 1964, the Arab leaders, prompted by the announcement of Israel's National Water Project, met in Cairo to consider retaliatory plans, even to the extent of diverting the headwaters of the Jordan away from Israel. The conference also adopted a programme of preparation for a future military showdown with Israel and this included the formation of a Palestine Liberation Organisation with its own armed forces. The 1956 Sinai Campaign had put an end to *fedayin* raids from Egypt, but similar activities by El Fatah terrorists began to infiltrate from Syria in the early 1960s. In May 1967 Nasser evicted the UN emergency forces from the Gaza Strip and Sharm el Sheikh, and recommenced a military build-up in Sinai. This coincided with an increase in border raids from Syria, Jordan and Lebanon and an escalation in the shelling of Jewish settlements. The smouldering conflict erupted into war on 5 June, but in less than a week Israel had destroyed the Arab air and ground strength in a series of military manoeuvres that have been described as the swiftest and most shattering feats of arms in history.

As a result of the Six Day War, Israel acquired an additional 26,500 square miles of territory, which covered the Sinai peninsula, the Gaza Strip and the Golan Heights, East Jerusalem and West Bank Jordan. This expanded territory meant that Israel stood behind much less vulnerable lines and the country's sense of security was stronger. The armistic boundaries of 1949 were swept away and the occupied areas were placed under Israeli military administration in lieu of a final peace settlement and negotiations with the Arabs for recognised and secure boundaries. There were signs that Nasser's

successor, Sadat, was interested in negotiations with Israel but
no peace settlement was forthcoming and the period following
the war was marked by a chain of violence in the form of terror
raids, bombings, assassinations and hi-jackings, spreading the
arena of conflict from the Middle East to cities and airports
around the world.

A major challenge to Israel's existence came with the Yom
Kippur or Day of Atonement War in October 1973. The military strength of both Syria and Egypt broke the myth of Israeli
invincibility and brought grave internal political problems to
Israel itself. Although Israel crossed the Suez Canal, occupied
Mount Hermon and drove the Syrians back to Damascus, the
campaigns were more protracted, especially against Syria, and
the Kissinger peace talks were subjected to heavy bargaining
before cease-fire agreements and demilitarised zones were put
into operation in the Suez and Mount Hermon areas. The
major economic result of these negotiations was Sadat's agreement to reopen the Suez Canal to both world and Israeli shipping. Since 1973, however, Arab terrorist raids into Israel,
accompanied by mass murders, have escalated, and Israel has
retaliated with equally violent air raids on Lebanese towns and
villages. The future of the occupied territories remains an
unanswered question, and the most contentious problems concern East Jerusalem and West Bank Jordan. The strategic advantages of holding the West Bank are clouded by its large
Arab population and the fact that this could never be assimi-
lated into the Israeli state. One answer to the political problem
of East Jerusalem is to turn it into an internationalised city. As
such it would cater for the finer feelings of Jewry, as of Moslems
and Christians, since it would reflect the cosmic significance of
all three. Jerusalem, however, was the supreme goal of Zionism
and the Israelis regard it as non-negotiable in any peace settlement. The fact that a Holy City of Islam is now under Jewish
rule is a bitter blow to Arab pride and a major thorn in the
search for peace.

2

The Country and the People

In spite of its small size the physical geography of Israel is surprisingly complex and contains almost all the major relief elements characteristic of adjacent countries, although generally on a much smaller scale and in somewhat subdued form. In the simplest of terms the country consists of a maritime plain of varying width—from 32 kilometres to a few hundred metres—bordering the Mediterranean, backed by dissected hill country which forms the uplands of Galilee, Samaria and Judaea. Southwards, and with increasing aridity, both the coastal zone and the uplands merge imperceptibly into the semi-arid and desert wastes of the Negev and Sinai. To the east, however, the physical boundary is abrupt and the structural and topographical depression of the Jordan and Arava valleys forms the traditional division between the Mediterranean-oriented Cisjordan (Palestine proper) and the eastern Transjordan. From a geographical point of view, the latter, with its uplands of Ammon, Gilead, Moab and Golan (formerly Syria), may be regarded as the 'backland' of the entire region.

In the north, the highly dissected ranges of the Lebanon are continued without interruption into Israel to form the rounded, but structurally complex, hills of Galilee. Upper Galilee offers great lithological and morphological contrasts and was formed by the faulting and uplifting of tilted blocks in geologically recent periods. Elevation averages around 600 metres, but its maximum is reached in Mount Meron (1,208 metres) northwest of Safad, the highest summit within Israel's 1948 boundaries. Traditionally, Upper Galilee is separated from Lower

Galilee by the east-west Bet Ha-Kerem valley and the deep gorge of the Amud stream which drains to Lake Kinneret. The

1 Huleh Valley
2 Amud Valley
3 Jezreel Valley
4 Haifa-Acre Plain
5 Mount Carmel
6 Sharon
7 Shephelah
8 Wilderness of Judaea

Israel: physical regions

lower section differs not only in altitude (175–350 metres) but also in its vegetation and milder climate.

The uplands of Galilee fall away steeply on three sides—on the east to the well-defined Jordan valley, on the west to the fertile lowlands centred on the Bay of Haifa, Acre and Nahariya, and on the south to the Vale of Esdraelon or the Jezreel Valley. The latter is an important north-west to south-east corridor linking the Bay of Haifa with the Jordan valley. It extends for 50 kilometres and reaches a maximum width of 10 kilometres. Formerly malarial and uncultivated, the Jezreel Valley is now intensively farmed and highly productive.

Southwards, the upland plateau extends for nearly 150 kilometres under a variety of regional names. This central section of hill country includes Samaria and Judaea (formerly part of Jordan) and consists of a broad upfold of rocks, chiefly limestone, which reaches a maximum elevation of 1,016 metres in Tell Asur, north-east of Ramallah. Samaria, centred on Jenin, Nablus and Ramallah, is structurally and topographically complicated and consists of a series of mountain blocks and ridges isolating internal basins and valleys, many of them fertile. Southwards it merges into the simpler and more compact structure of the Judaean Uplands which form a strongly defined ridge. Judaea, with its chief towns of Jerusalem, Bethlehem and Hebron provides a barer, more open landscape and merges in the south-east into a semi-arid area of badland topography (the Wilderness of Judaea) bordering the western shores of the Dead Sea.

To the south of Hebron the uplands fall in altitude to the plateau and basin area of the Negev which averages 300–450 metres in elevation. In the east it is bounded by the steep cliffs of the Wadi Arava, but westwards and southwards it passes into the Sinai Desert proper. Much of the Negev is steppe or semi-desert, the traditional home of nomads, but irrigation projects have transformed large areas of potentially productive soils into rich agricultural lands. This is Israel's frontier region and the capital, Beersheba, is a rapidly expanding town. Further growth points are the mineral-extracting centres and the port and holiday town of Eilat at the head of the Gulf of Aqaba.

The River Jordan lies in a graben or structural depression which extends more than 450 kilometres from beyond the Lebanese border, through the Dead Sea and Wadi Arava, to the Gulf of Aqaba. Elevations steadily decrease from 80 metres near the source of the river to 790 metres below sea level on the floor of the Dead Sea. Between the borders of Lebanon and Lake Kinneret the Jordan flows through the Huleh valley, which prior to 1958 was a region of swamps and stagnant lakes.

Drainage and reclamation have now transformed the rich allu-
vial soils into one of Israel's most prosperous agricultural regions. South of the Huleh valley the river falls 260 metres in
elevation over a distance of 44 metres and enters Lake Kinneret
(Sea of Galilee, Lake Tiberias). This occupies a tectonic depression in the valley floor and the level of the lake lies 213
metres below sea level and reaches a depth of over 40 metres.
Prior to 1967, the Huleh and Kinneret regions lay on Israel's
frontiers with Syria. The country now administers the strategic
Golan Heights to the east and in the Yom Kippur War was successful in extending its military influence north-eastwards to
Mount Hermon (2,814 metres).

The section of the Jordan between Lake Kinneret and the
Dead Sea is known as the Ghor and to the south of Jericho the
valley reaches its maximum width of 22 kilometres. The flood-
plain is covered with dense gallery vegetation and the river
flows in tortuous meanders before entering the Dead Sea. With
a surface level of 400 metres below sea level and a further depth
of 404 metres, this is the lowest spot on the earth's surface.
Intensive water evaporation provides Israel with a rich mineral
reservoir and the extraction of a variety of salts is a major enterprise. South of the Dead Sea the structural continuation of the
Jordan valley is provided by Wadi Arava. The level of the floor
gradually rises to about 200 metres above sea level at the
watershed between the Dead Sea and the Red Sea and its main
function is that of a transport link between northern Israel and
Eilat.

The third basic division of Israel is also the country's economic heart, containing the major part of the population, farm-
lands and industries. Between the central uplands and the
Mediterranean a low-lying coastal plain stretches from Haifa
to beyond Gaza. In the north it is closely hemmed in by Mount
Carmel (546 metres), a spur of the Samarian uplands. Southwards it opens out to the Plain of Sharon, Israel's most densely
settled and most intensively utilised agricultural region.
Sharon's southern limit is the Yarkon river which reaches the
Mediterranean at Tel Aviv. Beyond Tel Aviv the plain again
becomes broader, but with a more arid climate and a sandier
soil. It corresponds with the ancient area of Philistia and

merges southwards with the extreme arid conditions of the Sinai peninsula. The junction between the southern coastal plain and the Judaean uplands is marked by a transitional foothill area of shallow basins and known as the Shephelah. Extending some 45 kilometres long by 15 kilometres wide, this area has been the scene of some of Israel's major rural development projects.

CLIMATE

Israel's climatic contrasts are related both to the country's great altitudinal variations and to the fact that it lies in a transitional zone between an 'extreme' Mediterranean climate and the desert margins. Differences are reflected in average rainfall totals which rapidly decrease southwards from 40in annually in Upper Galilee to 10in in the northern Negev (a traditional criterion for a desert climate) and 1·2in at Eilat. The rainy season, associated with the passage of Mediterranean depressions, lasts from mid-October to the beginning of May, but 70 per cent of all precipitation falls in December, January and February, and June, July and August are true drought months throughout much of the country. Weather stability during the dry season is associated with air masses of tropical origin and temperatures continue to rise to a maximum in August, although there are marked regional differences and diurnal changes caused by topography and land and sea breezes. Summers are extremely hot throughout the coastal plain. August temperatures in Tel Aviv vary between 72° and 86°F and the fact that it is a damp heat makes conditions all the more enervating. Jerusalem's climate is more tolerable (66–82°F in August) and its altitude assures a dry heat and cool nights. Summer temperatures in the Jordan valley steadily increase southwards and at Eilat they frequently exceed 100°F. Both Eilat and the Lake Kinneret areas, however, are much visited winter resorts where January temperatures range from 52° to 73°F and from 50° to 65°F, respectively. Winter temperatures reveal similar latitudinal and altitudinal differences and, whereas Jerusalem can experience several inches of snow and

Galilee several feet, freezing conditions are infrequent in the coastal lowlands. January temperatures for Tel Aviv vary between 52° and 68°F.

One special feature of Israel's climate is the high annual intensity of insolation which amounts to 75 per cent of the possible total hours of daylight. This large amount of solar energy is the main cause of the high evapo-transpiration rate which compounds the country's water shortage. On the other hand, the high intensity of sunshine is an asset to many branches of agriculture and benefits the tourist industry. Solar energy is being harnessed by modern technology and a frequent sight in Israel, especially in the coastal plain, are roof structures for the solar heating of homes and water.

FLORA AND FAUNA

Israel's range of plant and animal life is among the richest and most varied in the world. This is related to the country's range of natural regions and to the fact that it is located at the meeting place of three major phyto-geographic areas—the Mediterranean, the Irano-Turanic and the Sahara-Sindic. In biblical times much of Palestine was forested, but centuries of clearing for cultivation and fuel supplies, and overgrazing, especially by the goat, has altered the ecological balance and character of the vegetation, as has the introduction of agricultural plants and fruit trees not indigenous to the area. Few of the ancient forests survive and those seen today have been planted in the last fifty years, chiefly by the Jewish National Fund. The Jerusalem (Aleppo) pine, the tamarisk, the carob and the eucalyptus are the chief species used in afforestation. Changes in vegetation have also affected the animal population, although Israel's fauna has not been studied as satisfactorily as its flora. There are approximately eighty-eight known species of mammals, several of which are carnivorous, including hyenas, jackals, wolves and wild cats. There are also gazelles, wild boar, mountain hare and porcupine, over 359 species of birds, 76 reptiles and 434 fresh- and salt-water fish.

POPULATION AND IMMIGRATION

With the birth of the state, Israel's doors were dramatically opened to immigration. Both the Proclamation of Independence and the Law of Return (1950) guaranteed the unrestricted admission of Jews and their automatic Israeli citizenship as fundamental principles of the state. Within a decade a million immigrants entered the country and the problems of coping with their immediate needs of food, housing, work and health, and of their cultural integration into a unified state, were the dominant features of Israel's public scene. In 1948, the country's population was 848,000; at the beginning of 1971 (excluding the administered areas) it was 3,021,600. Of these, 2,561,400 were Jews, making Israel the world's third largest Jewish community, exceeded only by the USA and the USSR. Israel's remaining population was made up of 343,900 Moslem Arabs, 77,300 Christians (mainly Arabs) and 39,000 Druzes and other minorities.

As well as accounting for rapid population growth and the increasing degree of urbanisation, immigration was also responsible for radically altering the ethnic composition of the developing state. In 1919, Palestine was 90 per cent Arab and the figure for 1940 was between 60 and 70 per cent. After 1948, largely for political reasons, the great majority of the Arab population left and in 1971 Israel's non-Jewish element accounted for only 14 per cent. This figure, however, was three times that of 1948, and the growth of the Arab sector is related chiefly to natural increase and improved health facilities and, to a much lesser extent, to the admission of relatives under the government scheme for reuniting families. It is interesting to note that if the populations of the areas occupied since 1967 are taken into account, the Jewish majority is greatly reduced. The reunification of Jerusalem alone added some 62,000 Moslems and 11,000 Christians; there are a further 616,000 Arabs in Judaea and Samaria, and 368,000 in the Gaza Strip and northern Sinai. These figures have been put forward as powerful arguments against Israel's permanent annexation of the administered areas. In 1970, 46·2 per cent of the Jewish population were native born (the Sabras); the remainder came from over 100 different countries: 27·5 per cent from Europe, America and Australia, 13·9 per cent from Africa and 12·4 per cent from Asia. Of the Sabra element, 17 per cent of their paternal parents were born in Israel, 36 per cent in Europe or the Americas, and 47 per cent in Africa and Asia.

Since 1948, the tide of immigration has ebbed and flowed as a result of political and economic conditions both within Israel and abroad. Up to 1960 it averaged 33,000 Jews per annum and during the next four years a formidable upsurge led to 220,000 new arrivals. In 1965–7 the yearly average dropped to 20,000, but since the Six Day War the curve has again been upward with totals of 32,679 in 1969, 36,928 in 1970 and 42,000 in 1971. What is often overlooked, however, is the number of Jews who have left Israel. Between 1948 and 1968, over 100,000 emigrated, and in some years the figure exceeded immigration. Most of those departing were originally from North America and Western Europe and were dissatisfied with the economic and social conditions that Israel could offer. Of the 35,000 who came from the USA and Canada in the 1940s and 1950s, only a small percentage remain.

Each phase of immigration has been characterised by the arrival of dominant groups. Between 1948 and 1950 more than half the immigrants were of European origin and were either the survivors of concentration camps or those released by the British from detention centres in Cyprus. Many came from East European countries where there seemed to be no future for the local Jewish communities, and these were complemented by Jews from the Arab countries of North Africa and the Middle East. 'Operation Magic Carpet' (1949) brought almost all the Jews from the Yemen by airlift from Aden and others came from Iraq in 1950–51—'Operation Ezra and Nehemia'. The Yemeni and Iraqi Jews totalled over 145,000, and in 1951 60 per cent of all immigrants originated from Asian countries.

The countries of origin changed considerably in the next decade. Between 1954 and 1958 over 80 per cent of immigrants came from North Africa and in 1957–60 Europe provided 50 per cent of the newcomers. North Africa was again the principal source region in 1962, and from 1964 onwards the majority originated from Europe and America. In recent years Soviet Jewry has made up a big proportion of the immigration and their claim to the right to settle in Israel has aroused worldwide sympathy. They represent what is perhaps the last great wave of immigration and, provided they are free to do so, it is estimated that a large section of Russia's three million Jews will eventually end up in Israel.

The Jewish Agency, in co-operation with the government, facilitates all aspects of immigration, including entry formalities, transient accommodation, vocational and professional training and employment. The majority arriving today are motivated not by tribulation and duress but by a voluntary decision to make Israel their home. Many have skills and professions, but still require individual attention preparatory to arrival and integration. Much of this advice and assistance is provided by the Jewish Agency's offices abroad. Within Israel the cost of culturally integrating a diverse population is high. The gap between Oriental Jews and those from the West, particularly in terms of education standards, professional skills and political thought, constitutes the country's main sociological problem. At the same time it is compounded by a substantial Arab population whose absorption into a unified state raises other major issues. The solution to these problems involves vast capital expenditure and this cannot be met, more than fractionally, by the internal resources of the country.

THE JEWISH POPULATION

In view of their vastly different homelands, it is a fallacy to regard the Jews as a homogeneous people. Israel's population is a rich tabloid of ethnic and cultural groups and there can be little justification for the idea of a Jewish race. By tradition, the Jews fall into two principal classes—the Sephardim and the Ashkenazim—which represent differences in geographical origin rather than in religious ritual, except in minor detail. Today, this subdivision is continued by the existence of two Chief Rabbis who govern on all religious matters from Hechal Shlomo, the seat of the Chief Rabbinate in Jerusalem.

The Sephardim are the descendants of the Jews who settled in the Iberian peninsula and from which they were expelled in the fifteenth century. Their language was Ladino, a Spanish dialect, and their name derived from Sepharad, a term applied by the Jews in the Middle Ages to Spain. The Sephardim were intellectually and materially far in advance of the Jews of north and central Europe, who were largely confined in physical and intellectual ghettos. In Palestine they settled in Safad, which they made the centre of Jewish mysticism, and in Jerusalem, re-laying its foundations as a centre of Jewish learning. Up until the early years of this century the Sephardim formed the largest section of Jews in Palestine and were accepted as the élite of Jewry.

Today, the term Sephardim has changed and is now used to denote any community of Jews which is not definitely Ashkenazim. Broadly speaking, the Sephardi Chief Rabbi has jurisdiction over oriental Jewish communities emanating from the Middle East and North Africa. Of these the Yemeni Jews are the best known and represent the descendants of Jewish tribes in Arabia which refused to accept Islam. Physically more akin to Arabs and with Arabic as their mother tongue, they arrived in Palestine as artisans and craftsmen, and founded villages on the outskirts of Haifa, Tel Aviv and Jerusalem. Other oriental communities include those of the Iraqi, Bokharan, Urfa, Persian and Georgian Jews, many of which settled in Jerusalem.

The Ashkenazim originate from Central and Eastern Europe, more particularly Germany (*Ashkenaz* in Hebrew), or are descendants of the Ashkenazim who emigrated to America, South Africa and other lands. Their language was Yiddish, a compound of Hebrew and Medieval German written in the Hebrew characters. They took the lead in Palestine's initial Jewish land settlement and formed the basis for the move to independence. The Ashkenazi Chief Rabbi is generally responsible for Western Jewish communities; Ashkenazim Jews, because of their 'modern European' ideas, have the major influence in Israel. The revival of the Hebrew language, how-ever, has been based on the Sephardic pronunciation of the Hebrew tongue.

These major divisions of Judaism have separate synagogues,

which differ somewhat in their ritual, but have no major doctrinal differences. It is significant that although, as a church, Judaism is notoriously disorganised and decentralised it is still more uniform in doctrine and observance than the various sects of Christianity and Islam. Judaism has no 'dogmas', and the basis of its belief is the incessant struggle to serve the will of God (Yahweh) in all things. However, there are definite rules which every believer must observe. They are contained in the Jews' holy scripture, the Torah (law), attributed to Moses (the five books of Moses, or Pentateuch). In addition there are commandments which are laid down in the collections Mishna (c AD 200) and Gemara (c AD 500). Mishna and Gemara collectively form the Talmud.

On the edge of Jewry, but not within it, are two other communities, both consequences of schisms in earlier centuries. The Karaites, who number about 10,000, live mainly within or near Ramla. The sect rejects rabbinical law and insists on a literal interpretation of the scriptures. The Samaritans recognise only the authority of the Torah and the Book of Joshua. Their numbers are small, being confined to Holon, near Tel Aviv, where there is a synagogue, and to Nablus, which is the residence of the High Priest. Mount Gerizim, near Nablus, is sacred to the Samaritans.

LANGUAGE

The revitalisation of Hebrew, which has restored it to the position of a living language, had its beginnings in the cultural renaissance led by Moses Mendelssohn towards the end of the eighteenth century. However, it was not until it became part of the nationalist Zionist movement for the return to Palestine that Hebrew passed beyond pure scholarship and literature. The Zionist leaders were aware that Jews drawn from all the lands of the Diaspora needed a common language and much of the credit for its development as a colloquial speech is attributed to Ben Yehuda who compiled the first dictionary of modern Hebrew. Succeeding generations of authors and scholars transformed the ancient tongue into a highly polished instrument of daily speech, literature, scholarship and science. The Hebrew Language Academy was established by law 'to direct the development of the language on the basis of research into its various periods and branches'. It continues the work of the Hebrew Language Council, founded in 1890. The Academy's decisions on matters of grammar, orthography, terminology and transliteration, published in the *Official Gazette*, are binding on educational and research institutions, as well as on government departments and local authorities.

Hebrew and Arabic are Israel's official languages, with English a semi-official lingua franca used widely but decreasingly in most public notices. Everyone speaks Hebrew a little differently and only a few experts are sure about what is really the correct pronunciation. Consequently newcomers to the language have a great deal of latitude, but an attempt at standardisation is made through a variety of intensive Hebrew language courses and other aids to help immigrants (see Chapter 7). Most Israelis, however, speak at least two languages; apart from Hebrew there is Arabic, English, German, French, Yiddish, Ladino and tens of other languages.

THE NON-JEWISH POPULATION

The bulk of Israel's non-Jewish population may be appropriately termed Arab, although there are a few to whom this appellation does not strictly apply. The Moslems form the largest group (343,900 in 1971) and can be assumed to be the descendants of Palestine's various ancient inhabitants. Within the country's pre-1967 boundaries, the largest concentrations are in Galilee and along the eastern margins of the Sharon plain. The largest Moslem urban communities are found in Nazareth, Haifa, Acre, Ramla and Lod. In addition, some 34,000 Bedouin live in Israel, most of them in the northern Negev, around Beesheba, but some are also found in Lower Galilee. Many Bedouin have seized upon opportunities of settling down and becoming farmers, but the majority still continue in their traditional pastoral nomadic way of life.

Israel's Moslems belong mainly to the Sunni sect and correspond to the majority of the Arab population of the Middle East. The Moslem community is largely autonomous in religious matters and officially is permitted to enjoy civic freedom and rights as citizens of the state. In the early days, and at times of Arab crises, internal security overrode these considerations. In 1971 there were over 200 Moslem clergy paid by the state and regular services were held in some ninety mosques. The Dome of the Rock and the el-Aqsa mosque in Jerusalem are the principal Moslem shrines, but other main centres are the el-Jazzar mosque in Acre and the new mosques of Haifa and Nazareth.

In Galilee there are some 1,200 Circassians living in the villages of Kafr Kama and Rehaniya. They are Moslems who were brought from the Caucasus Mountains in the nineteenth century by Sultan Abdel Hamid. The Druzes are another colourful minority. They broke away from Islam in the tenth century and have been granted the status of an autonomous religious community in Israel. The 38,000 living in villages in Galilee and Mount Carmel have been augmented by a further 8,000 in the Golan Heights.

In 1971, the Christian communities, mainly Arabs, numbered 77,300. They belong to thirty denominations, the principal ones being Greek Catholic (25,000), Greek Orthodox (22,000), Latin (16,000) and Maronite (3,500). In addition there are around 2,500 Protestants (Anglicans, Presbyterians, Baptists and Lutherans), and 3,500 adherents of the Eastern Monophysite Churches (including Armenian, Coptic, Ethiopian and Syrian Orthodox). Over 11,000 Christians live in Jerusalem, which is the seat of the Greek Orthodox, Latin and Armenian Patriarchs, and the site of many of the Holy Places of paramount importance to Christendom. The spiritual and religious centre of the Baha'i faith is also in Israel. In spite of its adherence to the teaching of Islam, this sect can no longer be considered Moslem. The founder of the sect was the Persian Ali Mohammed and its aim is the creation of a world religion which could be described as 'philanthropic monotheism'. The principal shrines are in Acre and Haifa; the latter's Universal House of Justice is situated on Mount Carmel.

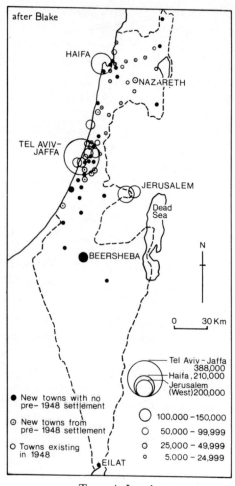

HAIFA

○NAZARETH

TEL AVIV-
JAFFA

JERUSALEM

Dead
Sea

N

●BEERSHEBA

0   30 Km

Tel Aviv – Jaffa
388,000
Haifa ,210,000
Jerusalem
(West)200,000

100,000 –150,000

50,000 – 99,999

25,000 – 49,999

5,000 – 24,999

● New towns with no
   pre– 1948 settlement

⊙ New towns from
   pre– 1948 settlement

○ Towns existing
   in 1948

EILAT

Towns in Israel

URBAN ISRAEL

Since 1948, there has been a rapid increase not only in
Israel's population but also in urbanisation. Today, Israel is
one of the most highly urbanised societies in the world, with
some 30 per cent of the population living in the three major
cities, Tel Aviv, Jerusalem and Haifa; 52 per cent in other
towns and cities, and 18 per cent in the countryside. In 1949 the
percentages were 48, 26 and 26 respectively; the outstanding

change is the higher proportion now living in the smaller urban centres. Planners have not so far been successful in reversing the trend of urbanisation, though a concerted policy of population dispersal is in operation.

The redistribution of population has been undertaken for both political and economic reasons. In 1948, 80 per cent of the Jewish population was concentrated in the coastal plain, especially in Tel Aviv and its immediate hinterland. Other concentrations were around Haifa and in Jerusalem, and these cities, especially Tel Aviv, presented vulnerable military targets. On the other hand, much of the south—70 per cent of the country—lay almost empty. On independence, Beersheba was a small market town for the Bedouin with a population of around 5,000 inhabitants. The Bedouin still go there, but with a population of 77,400 Beersheba today represents a regional capital in the true sense of the word, providing important services for the whole of the Negev.

Israel must be regarded as one of the world's laboratories of new-town development. Other centres of the south, created and planned according to the policy of population dispersal, are Ashkelon and Ashdod. The former (pop 40,000 in 1971) was created from the amalgamation of an immigrant reception centre in the abandoned Arab township of Majdal and a seaside resort. Ashdod (37,000 in 1971) is planned as the central town of the Judaean coastal plain and its selection as the site of Israel's second Mediterranean port has greatly aided its expansion. Two smaller towns, Yavne (8,000) and Kiryat Malakhi (7,000), are being planned as intermediate links in the new hierarchy. The other main areas of new-town development are Galilee and the north coastal plain.

The same deliberate policy of inducing immigrants to settle in peripheral areas has characterised rural settlement. The first and largest regional grouping was set up in 1955 in the Lachish area of the Hebron foothills. The plan is based on collective settlements (see pages 41–2) and the villages of fifty to ninety families focus on a rural centre which includes a school, clinic, primary marketing facilities and an agricultural machinery centre. The rural centres in turn focus on the main town of Kiryat Gat (18,000). Similar regional projects have been developed at Taanach, south of Afula, and at Adullam in the Jerusalem corridor.

In spite of these major efforts to disperse the population, few fundamental changes have been achieved. The pull of the heartland and the economic and social dominance of the Tel Aviv conurbation remain stronger than government incentives for the attraction of population to other regions.

Tel Aviv

There is a story that an Israeli politician, when asked the population size of Tel Aviv, responded, 'Do you mean this morning or this evening?' The ungainly, sprawling giant of a commercial capital, undreamed of sixty-five years ago, was born as a suburb of Arab Jaffa and grew to be the first and the largest all-Jewish city in history. The municipality (population 384,000 in 1971), which includes the old city of Jaffa—the biblical Japho or Joppa—is the core of an extensive conurbation with a population approaching 1 million, a figure equivalent to one-third of the country's total, and one-half of the country's urban population. The built-up area incorporates an inner ring of towns, including Ramat Gan (115,500), Benei Beraq (72,000), Giv'atayim (46,000), Bat Yam (83,500) and Holon (88,500), together with an outer ring of centres which are also an integral part of the conurbation. These stretch from Ra'anana and Kefar Sava in the north, through Petah Tiqva and Lod, to Ramla and Rehovot in the south. The entire area constitutes a continuous urban region with a distinctive geographical uniformity, both in terms of morphology and economic structure.

As a residential suburb of Jaffa, Tel Aviv was founded in 1909, two kilometres north-east of the old town on a site of unutilised sand dunes. Arab Jaffa was cramped and insanitary, and the new Jewish quarter was originally planned as a garden suburb within commuting distance of the town. In 1910 it was given the name Tel Aviv (Hill of Spring) and it became the nucleus around which a new city was to flourish. Growth was spectacular as Tel Aviv was a great attraction for new immigrants who brought in skills and capital. From a population of 13,000 in 1922, it grew to 34,000 in 1925 and to 120,000 in 1935 when it became the largest urban centre in Palestine. Prior to the outbreak of World War II Tel Aviv had established itself as the Jewish 'capital' and it became the initial seat of government with the foundation of the state. The transference of government to Jerusalem in no way undermined the city's commercial significance and by 1950 it had annexed the old port city of Jaffa.

Today, Tel Aviv-Jaffa is the economic and cultural nerve-centre of Israel, but like all large metropolitan areas it faces critical problems. Here are to be found the most wretched of Israel's poor, many of whom live in shelters made of cardboard boxes and tin cans. Their lot contrasts with the plush suburbs of Herzliya and Savyon. It also suffers from imminent traffic paralysis and its redevelopment problem, consequent to the speed of its growth, is the most pressing in Israel. In short it is a modern commercial metropolis with all the problems and inconsistencies this term evokes.

Jerusalem

Jerusalem is to Tel Aviv what Edinburgh is to Glasgow or Ottawa is to Toronto and Montreal. Jerusalem is Israel's historical and political capital and in a sense a national rival to the commercial predominance of Tel Aviv. Today its population is 304,500, but until 1967 it was divided into Jordanian and Israeli sectors (East and West Jerusalem), with the Old City, the Mount of Olives, Mount Scopus and most of the northern suburbs as part of Jordan. The modern city grew up mainly west of the Old City and covered a much larger area, with wide streets and modern buildings in contrast to the narrow and crooked lanes within the old walled city. Prior to 1967 West Jerusalem was linked to the rest of Israel by a narrow corridor and the city was surrounded on three sides by Jordanian territory.

The Israelis have made it clear that they will never accept a re-division of Jerusalem and the city is now undergoing its greatest metamorphosis in 2,000 years. A master plan has been developed that will transform the city's face and more than double its population. This is viewed with some alarm by the preservationists who see rapid development as ruining its character. High-rise office buildings and housing projects are in danger of destroying the vista of the Old City, but within its walls the twisting alleys, bazaars and religious shrines remain unaltered. The Old City also retains its traditional division into Moslem, Armenian, Christian and Jewish quarters which surround the chief religious sites of these faiths, although the Jewish quarter was evacuated between 1948 and 1967.

For all its modernisation Jerusalem remains a city of anomalies. It has more old people than any city in Israel, yet its birth rate is double that of 'young' Tel Aviv. It has a large number of people with academic degrees, but an unusually high proportion of illiterates. The city, as the Jewish capital, has more Christian denominations than Rome, together with a large number of religious zealots and anti-zealots.

Haifa

There is a saying in Israel that, when Tel Aviv plays and Jerusalem studies, Haifa works. The analogies are obviously exaggerations, but it is a fact that to the Israelis Haifa is known

---

Jerusalem is Israel's historical and political capital. The Old City is dominated by the domes and spires of the major religious shrines. Beyond rise the modern buildings of New (West) Jerusalem, the essential core of the state.

Tel Aviv is a product of the twentieth century and today it is Israel's largest city and the country's commercial, industrial and entertainment centre. Often described as the suburb of a non-existing city, Tel Aviv is now engaged in a comprehensive programme of redevelopment.

as the 'Workers' City', mainly because its inhabitants are occupied in the diverse industries that have developed either within
Haifa's boundaries or in the nearby bay-side area. Oil refineries, foundries, glass, textiles, fertiliser plants, car assembly
works etc, not to mention the activities of the port, give to the
city a more sober, steady character than that of the pre-
dominantly commercial metropolis of Tel Aviv. Although in-
dustrialisation may have detracted somewhat from Haifa's
aesthetic appearance, its inhabitants are convinced that they
live in Israel's most beautiful city. The chief tourist attraction is
the magnificent view over the harbour and bay to the north
from the slopes of Mount Carmel, which dominate the city.
Haifa owes its well-kept appearance and cleanliness to its
former mayor, Aba Khoushy, who waged a life-long campaign
against litter and drabness. To Tel Avivians Haifa is
straitlaced—'a moral curfew', as one writer has put it. Even so,
it is the only city in Israel where public transport runs regularly
on the Sabbath, in spite of the protests of the orthodox community.

With a population in 1971 of 217,400, Haifa is Israel's main
port (see Chapter 6) and the metropolitan centre of the north.
Like Tel Aviv, its growth is largely the product of this century

———

The Negev desert is Israel's frontier region and greatest challenge. Its
strange geological formations, stark scenery and great altitudinal variations make it a foremost tourist attraction. The Negev also holds the
story of Israel's past and is a rich reserve of mineral deposits.

Water is the key to life in the desert. At Ein Gedi, near the banks of the
Dead Sea, cucumbers are grown under plastic covering as a protection
against extreme heat.

and the heterogeneous population reflects both the development of the city as a mixed Jewish-Arab centre and the influx of immigrants into modern Israel. The port facilities, naval base and oil refineries are chiefly the work of the British, who recognised the importance of Haifa as a Mediterranean gateway to south-west Asia. The great wave of immigration began in the 1930s, and during and shortly after World War II Haifa became the centre of illegal Jewish entry into British-mandated territory. After 1948, as elsewhere in Israel, the population of Haifa grew rapidly to its present total and a number of municipally independent but economically integrated settlements grew adjacent to the city, with a further population of around 102,000. Haifa developed rapidly to keep pace with Israel's economic growth, but today the city suffers from being peripherally situated to the country's main centre of gravity. As a result it has to be content with the role of regional centre for the north.

RURAL SETTLEMENT

Israeli rural settlements are as diverse as the country's population. They reflect local geographical factors, the origin of settlers and, above all, their ideologies. The Arab village is the only form of rural settlement that follows a tradition of centuries. It was originally sited for reasons of security and water supply with the layout determined by the Moslem laws of inheritance and land classification. Many Arab villages are hilltop settlements of closely packed stone and mud houses, intersected by a maze of narrow, crooked lanes. The majority consist of two or more densely populated quarters separated by belts of open ground, the traditional area of the market and other communal activities. Today, Arab villages are connected by metalled roads to the national network and they have reached a degree of prosperity previously unknown. The outward signs of progress are new schools, clinics, piped water supplies and television aerials. Arab agriculture remains backward, but other changes include reclamation projects, marketing schemes and the scientific training of farmers.

Although the first Jewish villages in Palestine bore morphological similarities to European examples, the majority of settlements are of types not found elsewhere in the world. At the beginning of this century, socialist ideas, and German and Danish ideas of land reform and co-operation, became connected with Zionist philosophy, especially among Eastern European Jews. Such groups, who settled in Palestine, became the founders of Merhavya and Deganya, the prototypes of Israel's collective settlements. Their principles included the national ownership of land, co-operation and mutual aid, and no hired labour. The collective structure of these communities compensated for the individual's lack of agricultural training and benefited land colonisation and reclamation.

Early in its formative stages the co-operative movement split into two main branches. One group chose the form of the strict collective settlement, the *kibbutz* (plural *kibbutzim*) or *kvuzah* (*kvuzoth*), while the other preferred the structure of the co-operative smallholding settlement, the *moshav* (*moshavim*). The first *moshav* was set up at Nahalal in the Jezreel valley in 1920. Its founders were a splinter group from Deganya. Both movements adhere to common principles of ownership and co-operation, but there are a number of ideological subdivisions. The degree of collectivisation influences not only the way of life and form of the settlement, but also the branches of agriculture in which each type specialises.

In its strictest form the *kibbutz* (derived from the Hebrew word meaning 'group') is a communal and collective village governed by the general assembly of all its members. Its structure is based on equality in everything: work, housing, food, clothing and the raising of children. The basic principle is that every member gives to the community to the best of his abilities and in return receives from it according to his needs. Apart from individual living quarters, which today consist of modern and well-equipped apartments, the communal motivation is apparent in the central dining room, kitchen and stores, children's quarters and social and cultural centres.

The *kibbutz* has earned a place in the annals of Israel's development and its history is inextricably bound up with land reclamation, swamp drainage, malaria fighting and guarding the country's borders. In the early days the *kibbutzim* formed pioneer outposts and were built in the standard 'stockade and tower' style. The early pioneering days are now gone, but the *kibbutzim* are still a secure foothold along the borders from the Golan Heights and Upper Galilee in the north to Sinai in the south. Almost all are based on mixed farming, though specialisation on certain crops and animals is common, and many run sizeable industrial enterprises. Today, however, the ideology behind the *kibbutz* movement is being questioned. Many see it as anachronistic and gradually its members, especially the younger element, are being drawn into the wider social, cultural and intellectual life that has developed nationally. Of Israel's 1,000 agricultural settlements, 236 are *kibbutzim*. These contain only 5 per cent of the country's population, but their contribution to agriculture cannot be overemphasised.

The term *moshav*, meaning a smallholders' village, is applied to a less rigidly organised community. A *moshav shitufi* is similarly based on collective ownership, but work and pay are adjusted to individual needs; each family has its own house and looks after its own cooking, laundry and children. In a *moshav ovdim* each member owns a farm or smallholding worked by himself and his family, but all produce is sold and all supplies and equipment bought on a co-operative basis. These settlements are sometimes called 'workers' co-operatives'. In 1972, there were 347 *moshavim* of various types with populations ranging from 100 to 1,000.

3

How the Country is Run

'The Israeli political scene, often raucous and noisy with the clatter of endless disagreement, can be acerbated, stifled, and maimed by tremendous personal rivalries, hatreds, antagonisms and fanatic loyalties. Yet within it there is often a strong quality of theatrical drama. For the duration of the show the actors assault and poison each other; at the same time they are animated by a common desire to make the show succeed and hold the public in its spell for long after'.

Amos Elon. *The Israelis*

A COUNTRY constantly threatened by war might be expected to have a uniform and settled domestic political scene. The fact is that Israel's internal politics have been no less stormy than the country's external relationships with Arab neighbours. The politically minded Israelis hold outspoken views about how their country should be run and endlessly complain that they are a misgoverned people. Recognising the importance of strong leadership representing the country as a whole, the demands they place on the government are exorbitantly high and they are quick to criticise their leaders, especially for indecisiveness and bending to minorities. The result has been a succession of governments and party leaders, resignations and reinstatements, political splinter groups and temporary party affiliations.

43

PRESIDENT AND CONSTITUTION

The country is a parliamentary democracy headed by a president who is elected, initially for five years, by the Constituent Assembly, the Knesset. Ten or more members of the Knesset may propose a candidate for the presidency and voting is by secret ballot. Israel's first president, elected on 16 February 1949, was Dr Chaim Weizmann, the former president of the World Zionist Organisation. He was succeeded on his death, in November 1952, by Itzhak Ben Zvi who was re-elected in 1957 and 1962. Ben Zvi was followed in 1963 by Shneur Zalmon Shazar (re-elected in 1968) and the current presidential successor is Ephraim Katzir, appointed in 1974.

The president is the formal head of state, but, unlike his counterpart in the United States, is not the head of the executive. His powers resemble those of a British constitutional monarch, representing the nation as a whole, and he is above party politics. Presidential duties, therefore, include the receiving of visiting heads of state and ambassadors, signing international treaties and formally appointing ministers, judges and Israel's representatives abroad. The president also has the prerogative of pardon and of commuting sentences.

Israel has no formal written constitution, only a series of basic laws enacted since the establishment of the state or inherited from the mandate. The Administrative Ordinance of 1948 was designed as a 'small constitution' and defined the main branches of government (the administrative, legislative and judiciary) and the Transition Law of 1949 presented in general terms the powers of the president, legislative and cabinet. The absence of a formal constitution is due to the acknowledgement, especially by the leadership of the largest secular party, Mapai, of the necessity to avoid a *kulturkampf* on the constitutional position of religious law which continues to govern issues of personal status, marriage and divorce. This implied the continuation of the *status quo* and the adoption of a state constitution over an unspecified period through the passing from time to time of fundamental laws. The rights of the individual are based upon the accepted principles of English Common Law and many of these safeguards were contained in the Proclamation of Independence and are now considered as part of a basic constitution.

THE KNESSET AND CABINET

Israel's supreme authority is the Knesset (literally 'assembly'), a single-chamber parliament of 120 members. It is elected by universal suffrage under proportional representation for four years, but may, by specific legislation, decide on new elections before the end of its official term. Israeli nationals over the age of twenty-one are eligible to stand for Knesset elections. Exceptions are the country's judiciary, religious officials, army officers, senior civil servants and holders of other high state offices.

Following a general election the president calls upon the leader of the largest political party (as indicated by the election results) to form the executive. Its relationship to the Knesset is much the same as that of the British government to the Houses of Parliament and in many important respects British parliamentary procedure is followed. The functions of the Speaker, elected by the Knesset, may be likened to his counterparts in both the House of Commons and the US House of Representatives and there are also Deputy Speakers, representing the main political parties. A house committee regulates the Knesset's proceedings and question-time has also become a standard feature of parliamentary practice. Again, as in Britain, a bill must go through three separate readings before it becomes law. Debates are conducted in Hebrew, but Arab members may address the house in Arabic, and there are simultaneous translations of Hebrew and Arabic speeches. The legislative procedure relies a great deal on committees chosen, as far as possible, to reflect the weight of party representation. They consider bills after their initial presentation to the full house and consider reports from ministers and senior officials.

The cabinet or government is the functioning executive body and is headed by the prime minister. It is directly responsible to the Knesset and takes office on receiving a vote of confidence from that body. Resignation of the prime minister is tantamount to the resignation of the whole cabinet, but it remains in power until a successor government is formed. In spite of numerous political rifts and resignations, there has always been continuity of administration. Israel's present Prime Minister, Yitzhak Rabin, is the country's fifth in twenty-six years, following David Ben-Gurion (1949–54), Moshe Sharett (1954–63), Levi Eshkol (1963–9) and Golda Meir (1969–74).

THE ELECTORAL SYSTEM

All Israeli citizens over the age of eighteen are entitled to vote and the electoral system is a remarkably pure form of proportional representation. Like the political parties themselves it originated in the pre-state period and its model was the electoral system of the short-lived Kerensky régime in Russia, which in the eyes of the pioneers appeared as the acme of democracy. Each party puts forward a list of candidates for the country as a whole, with any number of names up to 120. The elector votes for the entire party list and the number of Knesset seats awarded is proportionate to the party's percentage of the total national vote, with a 1-per-cent minimum. For example, if a party polls 12 per cent of the votes it will be allocated 12 per cent of the Knesset seats, that is ten.

This system, which treats the country as one constituency, has both advantages and disadvantages. It is democratic in principle, but produces a multiplicity and often self-duplication of political parties at all general elections. This has the inevitable result of making it extremely difficult for any party to obtain a workable majority and necessitates coalition governments, the chief reason for friction in Israel's political scene. Ben-Gurion, Sharett, Eshkol, Meir and Rabin have had to negotiate, after each general election, on the terms on which they could establish a working majority. Another disadvantage of the system is that the elected becomes the servant of the party secretariat, rather than of the constituent, which makes it difficult for an Israeli to air a grievance without, as one writer recently put it, 'staging a riot'. Electoral reform is often spoken of, particularly the introduction of twenty or more constituencies which would help to reduce the number of political splinter groups and make representation more personal.

POLITICAL PARTIES

Almost every nuance of public opinion is represented in Israel's twenty or so political parties, yet although they may differ on internal affairs there are certain basic principles common to all platforms. These include the safeguarding of Israel's security and sovereignty, the maintenance of its military boundaries, the unity of Jerusalem, close ties with world Jewry through the Zionist Movement, and rapid economic and social development for the country. The one exception is the Naturei-Karta 'party' (a Hebrew-Aramaic term meaning 'Watchmen of the Town'), a small group of religious extremists living mainly in the Mea Shearim quarter of Jerusalem. They refuse to recognise the State of Israel and its government and participate little in the activities of the country.

Since the bulk of immigration has been from socialist lands, or where socialism was the opposition to tyranny, the dominant parties in Israel are labour parties. Their political significance is made stronger by the fact that the agricultural worker was also a socialist pioneer, and not, as in many countries, associated with the defence of the *status quo*. In Israel, therefore, there is little 'conservative' opinion, except in the case of the religious parties. The Israel Labour Party was founded in January 1968 by the Union of the Israel Workers' Party (established 1930), the Union of Labour (1944) and the Israel Workers' List (1965). Most of the important political personalities in Israel are connected with this group, which has held power without interruption since the establishment of the state. This, however, has necessitated frequent alignments and coalitions, including that with the United Workers' Party in 1969—a Zionist socialist party supported by the *kibbutzim*. The next largest grouping is the Herut-Liberal Bloc, founded in 1965 by agreement between the Herut (Freedom) Movement and the Israel Liberal Party. Herut is opposed to socialism and is strongly orientated towards the West. It strives to establish Israel within its historical borders, that is, the whole of the former mandated territory, and fights for the evacuation of Jews from Iraq, Syria,

Egypt, Russia and all other countries of anti-semitic outlook.

Israel's religious parties are equally diverse but all press for the adherence to the traditions of Judaism. A number are combined in the National Religious Party (established in 1956), labour's traditional coalition partner until 1974. It strives to establish the constitution of the country on Jewish law based on the ethical and social principles of the Torah and it is the political voice of the Chief Rabbinate. Agudat Israel and Poalei Agudat Israel hold more extreme views on the place of Judaism in the modern state. The country's Communist Party was founded in 1919 and its aims include non-alignment and recognition of the rights of Palestinian Arabs. In 1965 a party split founded the New Communist List with a foreign policy of neutrality and friendship with the Soviet Union and all socialist states.

Largely because of Israel's plethora of political parties and sectional interests no attempt is made to trace the controversies and domestic issues centred around personalities and parliamentary alignments. It should perhaps be stressed that the conflict between the secular and religious standpoint has been fundamental and has rocked many governments. Central to this has been the administrative definition of 'Who is a Jew' and the controversy was responsible for the withdrawal of the National Religious Party from the Labour coalition in 1958. The question remains unsolved since the rabbinical interpretation of Jewish parentage differs from the less orthodox viewpoint. Alleged political and military blunders have also been major bones of contention, as illustrated in the case of Pinhas Lavron, the Minister of Defence in Sharett's government. Many would argue that the collapse of Golda Meir's government, in spite of the exoneration of Moshe Dayan, was the result of Israel's heavy military losses in the Yom Kippur War. Israel's democracy, however, as the only true example in the Middle East, works well. Sectional interests are seen by the Israelis as an essential part of life and elections have the risks, the excitements and unpredictability of a roulette table. The old joke about the Jew who, when stranded on a desert island, founded two synagogues so that he could resign from one or the other of them, seems to summarise Israel's political situation.

NATIONAL INSTITUTIONS

A unique feature in Israeli life and in the running of the state is the part played by Jews abroad who are profoundly involved in the country's progress. The rationale for considering institutions such as the Jewish Agency, the Foundation Fund (the financial arm of the Agency), the Jewish National Fund and the Zionist Organisation as part of general government is that they were initially set up to undertake many government functions and laid the foundations of the country's independence. The mandate recognised the Zionist Organisation, and later the Jewish National Fund, as the principal representatives of Jewish interests in Palestine and, although some of their departments were abolished or curtailed with the creation of the state, not all activities were transferred to the government. The appropriate bodies continue to play an important financial role in the development of the country and co-operate with the government on behalf of Jews throughout the world.

The role of the Zionist Organisation, which had fought for the creation of a Jewish homeland in Palestine, secured by law, was redefined at the first Zionist Congress in independent Israel, held in 1951. The movement adopted the 'Jerusalem Programme' which covered immigration, settlement, fundraising and the fostering of Jewish education and culture in the Diaspora, and its relationship with the state was governed by the World Zionist Organisation Status Law of 1952. A new 'Jerusalem Programme' was formulated by the 27th Congress in 1968, and the Organisation's budget for 1971–2 was £11·4 ($26.2) million. Of this total, £4·0 ($9.3) million was spent on immigration, £2·5 ($5.8) million on youth and pioneering movements, £1·8 ($4.2) million on education and culture, and £3·1 ($6.9) million on administration and information.

Labour Zionism, an intermingling of Zionist and socialist ideals, has played an important part in the Zionist movement. The basic philosophy of Labour Zionism has been the development of a national home along socialist lines, that is, pioneers seeking to forge a Palestine as a result of their own manual labours. In 1920, the Federation of Labour (the Histadrut) was formed which sought to provide employment for Jewish workers, providing at the same time mutual aid and trade union protection (see Chapter 5). The Histadrut developed as a multi-purpose organisation representing the majority of Jewish workers and negotiating terms of employment. It departed radically from usual trade union practice in its entrepreneurial activities which became numerous and complex, dominating almost every branch of the economy. Politically, the Histadrut acquired positive, if indirect, influence, as control was through the same labour parties active in both the government and the labour movement. Today, almost without exception, all members of the labour parties are also Histadrut members and there is much truth in the adage that in Israel the workers have a Histadrut and the Histadrut has a government.

The Jewish Agency was founded in 1929 when the League of Nations Mandate for Palestine stipulated that there should be a recognised public body to co-operate with the administration on Jewish affairs. After 1948 its political functions disappeared, but the Agency continued as a para-governmental body with its practical functions in the fields of immigration, land settlement, housing, health, education and youth welfare. Since independence over £1,300 ($3,000) million has been spent, and the Agency has brought almost 1·5 million Jews to Israel and established over 450 villages. It is financed by voluntary contributions raised by the United Israel Appeal in the United States and the Keren Hayesod, the latter established in 1920 and operating in sixty-three countries.

A notable branch of the Jewish Agency is the Youth Aliyah which was founded in 1934 to rescue children from Nazi Germany. Since its inception it has brought over 140,000 children to Palestine from eighty countries. Recently the movement has been adapted to care for and train children of immigrant families, and over 9,000 children and young people are at present receiving academic, vocational and agricultural education in villages and institutions. A further 2,500 attend day youth centres.

Keren Kayemeth le-Israel (the Jewish National Fund) is

responsible for land development in Israel. It was founded in 1901 to acquire land for Jews in Palestine and until 1960 was the owner of all national land. The Fund has reclaimed over 200,000 acres of land, planted over 100 million trees, built 1,800 miles of roads in frontier and mountain areas, and contributed considerably to Israel's security.

JUSTICE AND THE LEGAL SYSTEM

Israeli law comprises a number of different systems and is still very much in a state of flux. When the British assumed the League of Nations Mandate in 1922, the law of Palestine was Ottoman, which in itself was based on Islamic and French law. The British introduced English Common Law and doctrines of equity into local jurisdiction, and much of this was kept by the independent state. The most notable amendments have taken place in criminal law and in 1950 the Nazi and Nazi Collaboration Law was passed to punish war crimes against the Jews and humanity. For this the death penalty is imposed, but has been applied only once in Israel's history in the execution of Adolf Eichmann. In 1950, corporal punishment and the death penalty for capital crimes was abolished.

Israel has no jury system, but the judiciary plays a fundamental part in the democratic structure of the state. The courts are independent of the executive, and judges are appointed by the president on the recommendations of an independent committee. The apex of the system is the Supreme Court of ten judges who are appointed for life. It sits in Jerusalem and also hears and decides appeals against district court judgements in both civil and criminal matters. The four district courts of Jerusalem, Tel Aviv, Haifa and Beersheba are composed of one or three judges who rule on all questions of fact and law. Below these are the magistrates courts which operate in all major towns and deal with minor matters, such as small monetary claims, less serious criminal charges and cases connected with land sale and purchase. They include special sections for juvenile and traffic offenders.

The judicial branch of government also comprises religious

courts which administer the traditional law of the Jews of the Diaspora, ruling in particular on matters concerning the personal status of Jews, especially marriage and divorce. The rabbinical tribunals are maintained by the Ministry of Religious Affairs, and their judges and officials are appointed by the president on the recommendation of a panel comprising rabbinical and lay members. The Jewish section of the Ministry is closely associated with the religious political parties and broadly supports their claims. As in the mandate, however, the civil courts execute the judgement of the religious tribunals which gives them the measure of control over rabbinical judges. Moslem and Christian courts have similar powers over personal status and Druze courts were established in 1963.

In the Beersheba area tribal courts also operate. Composed of Bedouin sheikhs appointed by the Minister of Justice, they deal with minor civil and criminal cases as long as the party concerned is Bedouin. Tribal law and court procedure follow local custom, but are controlled by, and geared to, the national justice and moral philosophy of the state.

LOCAL GOVERNMENT

Much of the framework of Israel's system of local government was inherited from the mandatory period, although many rural district councils have been created since independence. The country's six major administrative districts: Jerusalem, Northern (capital, Nazareth), Haifa, Central (Ramla), Tel Aviv and Southern (Beersheba) are further divided into 29 urban municipalities (two of which are Arab), 118 local councils (47 either Arab or Druze), and 48 regional councils to which representatives are sent from a total of 695 villages. In the occupied territories there are few Israeli administrative officials and the 28 town councils and 31 rural councils of the West Bank, for example, have the same mayors and representatives as under Jordanian rule.

Municipal elections follow the pattern of the Knesset elections and are usually held at the same time. Cities and regions are not divided into wards, but each party again submits its own list and the elector votes for a group of people rather than for an individual. The best an individual can do is to present himself as a one-man party and a number of local government officials have been returned in this way.

The local authorities are responsible for education, road maintenance, water and sewage, social services, health and sanitation, public parks and fire brigades etc. Their work is generally supervised by the Ministry of the Interior who approves budgets, rates and bylaws. Many local authorities have combined into larger municipal unions to look after educational, agricultural and hospital services.

THE CIVIL SERVICE

The civil service holds a peculiarly strong position in Israel. It is headed by a commissioner, appointed by the cabinet, and who is responsible to the Ministry of Finance. In principle it is non-political, but it is not uncommon for senior posts to go to the members of the party from which the responsible minister has been drawn. The creation of a competent civil service has been a difficult task, for only a small number of people had served in the mandatory government. Many civil servants have been recruited from the Public Service College in Jerusalem, which was founded by the Jewish authorities during the British period. This source of recruitment greatly eased the administrative problems consequent on the abrupt change to statehood. Today preference is given to university graduates and most senior posts are reserved for them. In 1971, civil servants, not including teachers, police and prison officers, numbered 55,170.

One of the most important and influential public offices in Israel is that of the State Comptroller. The appointment, for an initial term of five years, is made by the president on the recommendation of the Knesset. The comptroller's functions involve the scrutiny of the public services—their legality, efficiency, economy and ethical integrity—thereby providing a highly effective check on public expenditure and standards. The accounts and activities of ministries, local authorities and public industries are also examined. The annual reports attract widespread press and public attention and carry an almost unchallenged authority, in spite of the fact that the position is deprived of executive power. In 1971, the State Comptroller was given the duties of an ombudsman.

POLICE AND PRISONS

Israel's police force is an efficient and highly centralised agency, modelled largely on British lines. It is controlled by an inspector-general from headquarters in Jerusalem. The strength of the force in 1972 was 12,850, including 1,200 Arabs and Druzes and some 1,200 women. The country is subdivided into three police districts centred on Jerusalem, Tel Aviv and Nazareth and these in turn are composed of sub-districts, stations and posts. A duty unknown to most police forces in the world is the guarding of military boundaries and frontier settlements. This is the task of the border police who work in co-operation with the army. Since 1967, the Israeli police have also been responsible for law and order in the administered areas and local Arab policemen, 90 per cent of whom served under Jordanian and Egyptian rule, have been recruited and

---

Israel's plural society is vividly revealed in the streets and ethnic quarters of Jerusalem. Life in the Old City has changed little over the centuries and the famous Arab *souks* house a variety of workshops, coffee houses, souvenir shops and money-lenders.

The Mea Shearim district of West Jerusalem is the centre of the Jewish Orthodox community. The inhabitants dress in the style of Europe's medieval ghettoes and live in strict observance of the traditional Jewish precepts.

retrained for these duties. By and large the police force maintains excellent relations with the public; there is no street patrol, and traffic control is on European lines, supplemented by a volunteer service.

The prison service forms a separate section and is under the supervision of a commissioner. The majority of prisons are well equipped with workshops and vocational training centres, and farming is a common occupation. Produce is sold in local markets and prisoners are paid a low wage which can be saved and made available on release. Prior to their detainment in a particular institution, every prisoner undergoes a medical, psychological and psychiatric examination.

NATIONAL DEFENCE

Israel depends for its survival on military prowess which means that the defence force is disproportionately large and expensive for the country's population size and area. The percentage of military personnel within the population vies with North Vietnam, North Korea and Taiwan as being the highest in the world; in 1973 defence expenditure accounted for more than 30 per cent of the national budget—£700 ($1,600) million

---

Israel has monuments to its past and to its future. At Hebron, in the Israeli-controlled West Bank, the Tomb of the Patriarchs is sacred to Jews and Moslems alike. The large mosque, adapted from earlier Christian shrines, is surrounded by a wall traditionally attributed to King Solomon.

Tel Aviv is contrast and juxtaposition. The Shalom Tower dominates the city's skyline and the 30-storey building with department stores, office accommodation and an observatory is Israel's equivalent of the Empire State Building.

out of a total of £2,000 ($4,600) million.

The defence force consists of a nucleus of commissioned and non-commissioned regular officers, a contingent called up for national military service under the Defence Service Law, and a reserve. The force was established in 1948, during the War of Independence, on the basis of the Haganah and other voluntary underground organisations that operated during the mandatory period, and of veterans of the Jewish Brigade and other units which fought for the Allies during World War II.

The main defence body is made up of conscripted recruits. Men reaching the age of eighteen are called up for three years and are liable for service in the reserves up to the age of fifty-five. Until they are forty, men report for thirty-one days' training annually, and, from then until they are fifty-five, for fourteen days. Single women are conscripted for twenty months' service and are liable for the reserves up to the age of thirty-four. According to the Institute of Strategic Studies in London, Israel has 30,000 regular soldiers and 85,000 conscripts, and is capable of mobilising a total force of 300,000 equipped and completely operational within seventy-two hours.

There is no inter-service rivalry between the army, the navy and the air force. A single general staff and a chief-of-staff commands all armed forces, but the army is by far the largest service and has built up a strong mechanised spearhead. Next comes the air force with very high professional standards, followed by the navy, the smallest service. The country is subdivided into northern, central and southern commands, each headed by a major-general, and territorial defence is based on a linked chain of villages along frontiers, each equipped with their local commands, weapons and ammunitions. Within the army, Nahal (Pioneering Fighting Youth) offers essential training for manning agricultural frontier villages. Gadna, with its land, air and naval sections, also organises training for youths between fourteen and eighteen years.

It is interesting that despite the numerical importance of Israel's defence force, the influence of army leadership on political decisions is small. Public opinion has always been alert to the potential dangers of militarism and this is constantly guarded against, almost as consciously as the Arab threat.

CURRENCY AND FINANCE

The monetary unit in Israel is the lira (pound) which is divided into 100 agorot. There are coins for 1, 5, 10 and 25 agorot, ½ and 1 lira and banknotes for 1, 5, 10, 50 and 100 lirot. In November 1974, the US dollar was equivalent to 5·65 lirot and the pound sterling to 13·90 lirot. Since 1967, the Israeli lira has also been the legal tender in the occupied areas.

The National Bank of Israel is the central bank of the state and the bank of issue, regulating the currency system and credit and banking facilities throughout the country. Israel also has twenty-eight commercial banks, fourteen credit co-operatives and thirty-five other financial institutions. The largest commercial banks are the Bank Leumi le-Israel, the Israel District Bank and Bank Hopoalim. Long-term credits are also provided by the Israel Agricultural Bank, the Industrial Development Bank and the Maritime Bank. The Post Office deals mainly with clearing operations, savings and money orders, and receives and makes payments on behalf of the government and the National Insurance Institute.

Israel's budget is annually presented to the Knesset for approval and consists of the ordinary budget and the development budget. The former is financed by taxes and covers the normal expenditure of ministries and the cost of training, welfare and services for new immigrants. Development revenue comes from savings, foreign loans, appeal funds and the State of Israel Bonds. Bonds were first floated in 1951 and there have been a further four issues. They have raised over £765 ($1,750) million from sales in the USA, Canada, Europe and Latin America and the revenue has been directed to such projects as the national water carrier, the expansion of dock facilities at Haifa and Eilat, and the construction of the port of Ashdod.

4

How They Live

ISRAEL is basically a welfare country competing in a capitalist world. In terms of economic progress, social services and standard of living it is closer to Western Europe than to conditions in the Middle East. This stems partly from the superior technical experience of the Israelis and partly from the large amounts of foreign aid, which has enabled the country to develop along Western lines. Material and social progress has been rapid, but every facet of government and voluntary effort has felt the effects of mass immigration, with the burden of the problem falling on the welfare institutions. In the face of other major financial needs, direct welfare grants are modest, but slowly and soundly the needed services are developing, though many problems await solution. The provision of adequate housing for an expanding population has received top priority, but not to the exclusion of other services, and it is significant that the standard of general health compares favourably with most Western countries. The major problem, however, is related to the great variation in standards found within the country's population. The European ideal of economic aid and social progress, on which Israeli life is based, is strange to the Oriental Jew whose philosophy is reflected in different attitudes to housing, health and welfare services.

HOUSING

Israeli housing can vary from a Bedouin tent in the Negev and Judaean deserts to a luxurious apartment flat or villa in the Rehavia district of Jerusalem or the northern and western suburbs of Tel Aviv. The contrasts between the spartan and the sophisticated are equally conspicuous within the urban areas, particularly in Tel Aviv, where suburbs of the upper echelon of Israeli society are often built alongside slum quarters which house old immigrant families and the worst of Israel's poor.

The physical problem of accommodating immigrants has been enormous and the expedients for solving it have been constantly improved as the result of trial and error. Immediately following the proclamation of independence, the government and the Jewish Agency were forced to house the newcomers in large transit camps where they waited for resettlement and work. Some of these were old immigrant and detention centres inherited from the mandatory régime; others were former barracks which had been used by the British army. The problem would have been more critical were it not for the availability of homes deserted by the Arab refugees. Towns emptied of Arabs, like Jaffa, Ramla and Lod, and such abandoned Arab villages that remained intact, were rapidly filled with Jews. Even so, the camp populations grew at an alarming rate and at the end of 1949 over 100,000 people lived under canvas.

In order to remedy the deficiences of the 'camp' system, the *maabaroth* plan was instituted in 1950. These were transitional work-villages, and the underlying idea was to bring immigrants straight to the places where work of some kind was immediately available. They were sited adjacent to towns, agricultural villages or development projects, and accommodation was provided in neatly designed aluminium, tin or canvas-walled huts. Although temporary in nature, schools, medical centres and other welfare facilities were part and parcel of the *maabaroth* and they were successful in directing immigrants away from Tel Aviv, Haifa and the congested coastal plan.

At the end of 1951, much of Israel's population lived in temporary housing and almost another decade passed before the backlog was worked off. Slowly the *maabaroth* were cleared away and pauses in the great influx of immigrants provided the opportunity to build thousands of permanent homes and to institute a new 'ship-to-settlement' scheme. This enabled immigrants, even before embarkation, to know exactly where their ultimate destination in Israel would be. Shortage of time, money and resources, however, resulted in the erection of permanent houses as quickly as possible and at the lowest cost. Consequently, the majority of dwellings were compact, functional and aesthetically unpleasing. This almost ruthless standardisation and the warehousing effect of masses of identical dwellings has continued to the present, and the majority of residential districts throughout Israel appear visually depressing.

Since 1948, over 680,000 homes or 70 per cent of the country's total stock have been completed, making Israel's rate of house construction the highest recorded for any nation in proportion to its inhabitants. There has been considerable private development, but the majority of homes have been built by the government through the Ministry of Housing or through associations working closely with the ministry. Over half the public housing has been built for immigrants and managed by Amidar, the government housing organisation. In 1971–2, £47 ($114) million out of a housing budget of £80 ($190) million was allocated to meet the needs of the large numbers of immigrants arriving from the free countries and the USSR. Israel is determined that the Russian Jews, who defied the strongest tyranny in the world, should have nothing but the best in the way of jobs and housing. Slum clearance, however, has not been able to keep pace with the growth of population, although systematic efforts to re-house non-immigrant sections of the population are being made. In particular, there is a concerted effort to end the serious overcrowding and to redevelop the large areas of substandard housing in Tel Aviv. The government also plans to provide suitable accommodation for 7,000 young couples a year.

The most common type of public housing is the four-storey block of flats which has proved to be the cheapest form of residential construction. High-rise flats, however, are common in Tel Aviv, Jerusalem and other centres where the cost of building land justifies their construction. Israel's large cement industry enables all construction to be carried out in concrete, whether in the form of blocks, in-situ casting or precast components. This in itself produces regularity and monotony in housing development and even Jerusalem's world-famous stone is not readily detectable from reinforced concrete. In recent years architects have attempted to vary the type and layout of dwellings, but there are obvious limitations to designing an aesthetically pleasing apartment block that will be rented at low cost. Outposts of individuality in housing development are largely related to private, rather than public, construction.

The quick, cheap and sometimes shoddy building means that housing renewal is a great problem. Housing officials have declared that many new estates often become slums in less than a year, and the difficulties in maintaining communal standards are compounded when flats house large families of African and Asian origin. The Amidar organisation has attempted to 'educate' residents and to stimulate communal responsibility, but the equivalent of the British 'coals in the bath' tale is all too common in Israel. Sociologists have found that home ownership produces better standards of maintenance and this lends support to the government policy of home ownership for everyone. In recent years home ownership has increased considerably and now covers 60 per cent of the population. A significant development in apartment blocks is the cooperation of householders and the formation of house committees for the provision of common services.

Buying a house, however, is as difficult in Israel as it is in Britain and the United States. A luxury apartment with four to five rooms costs anything from £54,000 ($125,000) to £70,000 ($160,000); a modest two-room dwelling with full facilities runs to £13,000 ($30,000), if it can be found. The rapid rise in land values and house prices has not been helped by Zionist newspaper advertisements urging Jews abroad to purchase a second home in Israel. In 1971 more than 11 per cent of investment in housing was made by foreign Jews, mostly Americans. This has become a sore point with Israelis struggling to find deposits on homes which have doubled in price partly as the result of foreign demand. Another area of resentment is the special housing privileges now received by immigrants. With temporary housing more or less obsolete, the state is in a position to offer newcomers attractive homes, tax exemptions and low-interest loans, none of which were available to earlier immigrants. They move directly to new houses in development towns and are provided with furniture and cooking facilities on loan and generally with a stock of food to supply the family for a week. The welcome given to new immigrants is thus tinged with resentment, especially towards the Russians who are far more demanding than their predecessors. The Russians often insist on being housed where they please and have staged sit-down strikes at Ben Gurion airport in protest over housing and employment.

With the exception of the scheme operating for immigrants, Israel has no mortgage system such as exists throughout the Western world. Israelis have to pay cash for new homes or to borrow money at usurious rates. At the same time, few contractors build for letting purposes and young married couples in particular, 20 per cent of whom live with their parents, find it extremely difficult to own their own home. In order to ease the situation the government operates special schemes to aid the ordinary family with home buying. The 'Saving for Housing' project was initiated in 1955 to offset the fear of rising building costs, and the value of the depositors' funds are linked to the cost of the home in the year the account was opened. The project has attracted thousands of savers and there are parallel schemes operating on modified terms, such as 'Housing for Young Couples'.

With the accent on economy in living quarters and on the rapidly escalating cost of housing, it follows that the majority of Israeli homes are small. A family occupying a four-roomed apartment is spaciously housed by the country's standards and most have to be content with two or three rooms. The average occupancy rate is two persons per room (compared with 0·66 in Britain), but among families of African and Asian origin this figure is doubled. Folding beds and convertible couches are ubiquitous furniture items in Israeli homes, and those with verandahs or terraces are generally equipped with semi-rigid curtains that transform them into extra bed-space at night. An Israeli dreams of the time when he will be able to retire for the night without first having to unfold his bed!

With a shortage of space the Israeli house cannot be over-furnished, which is perhaps an advantage for even the poorest quality furniture is expensive by Western standards. In terms of modern facilities and domestic appliances, however, homes are well supplied. Seventy per cent of the housing stock has been completed since 1948, which means that 80 per cent of homes have a fixed bath or shower and an inside WC. In 1970, 90 per cent of families had ranges and ovens for cooking and baking, 75 per cent had refrigerators, 23 per cent washing machines, 16 per cent electric food mixers and 12 per cent vacuum cleaners. For entertainment, 92 per cent of all families had radios and 25 per cent record-players.

NATIONAL INSURANCE

In 1954, Israel introduced the National Insurance Law as part of a comprehensive social plan to combat poverty and build a progressive modern society. In many respects the system is similar to that of Britain and there are reciprocal arrangements between the two countries permitting rights acquired in one to be transferred to the other without loss of benefits. Housewives may also participate in national insurance which provides old-age pensions, survivors' insurance, maternity benefits and family allowances. There are also pensions and grants for disabled workers, and for families of breadwinners killed in work accidents.

The whole scheme is administered by the National Insurance Institute and is financed by the government, the employer, employees and self-employed persons. The following ratios in respect to incomes operated in 1972:

Contributions as percentage of income

	Work injuries	Old age and survivors	Maternity insur:	Family allow:	Equalisation fund	Unemployment insur:	Total
Wage Earners	—	1.6	0.3	—	0.6	1.0	3.8
Employers	1.2–4.5	4.5	0.6	2.8	3.2	3.0	15.6–18.9
Self-employed	0.5	4.5	0.6	2.3	1.2	—	9.4

The employers percentage contribution to work injuries varies according to the degree of risk in the undertaking, and to each total contribution (wage earners, employers and self-employed) a further 0·3 per cent defence tax is added. During the first sixteen years of operation, contributions amounted to some IL3,570 (£352 or $850) million, and benefits paid out exceeded IL2,651 (£259 or $630) million. About 2,717,000 cases have been dealt with: 1,027,000 employment injuries; 1,189,000 maternity insurance; 312,000 old age and survivors; 139,000 relating to large families.

In 1972, old-age pensions ranged from IL80 (£7·80 or $19) to IL270 (£25 or $64) per month according to family circumstances and other resources of the pensioner. Men receive pensions at sixty-five if they retire from work, otherwise at seventy. The corresponding ages for women are sixty and sixty-five. Receipt of a pension allows for the continuation of part-time employment for those who desire it. Survivors' insurance is payable on a sliding scale according to the number of children and the age of the widow.

Work injury insurance, which covers medical treatment and vocational rehabilitation, amounts to 75 per cent of wages and salaries paid for a period up to twenty-six weeks. Grants are also awarded for certain industrial injuries and burial expenses are included. Maternity benefits cover hospital expenses and a grant for a layette. In 1972 the amount was IL320 (£31·50 or $76) (IL220 for hospitalisation and IL100 towards the baby's clothes and equipment). Working mothers also receive twelve weeks' maternity leave at 75 per cent of their salary. The grants for hospital costs have had a desirable side-effect in that the percentage of babies born in hospitals has increased, with a consequent drop in the rate of infant mortality. Monthly family allowances are paid for children under eighteen, after the second child; IL22·50 for the third, fourth and fifth, and IL20 for the sixth and each additional child. Wage-earners also receive IL17·50 per month for each of the first two children and ex-servicemen receive extra allowances for each child after the third.

The National Insurance Institute also administers an unemployment fund and an equalisation fund for payment of wages to reservists called up for military duty.

SOCIAL WELFARE

Social problems in Israel have been aggravated by the aftermath of mass immigration, and the heavy financial burdens of defence, development and housing have seriously limited the resources available for welfare services. The basic responsibility rests with the Ministry of Social Welfare, though the Jewish Agency, the Zionist Organisation and the Histadrut are also active in the field. The social services are run by central and local authorities and the ministry co-ordinates, supervises and subsidises all public and voluntary work. Programmes include care of families, the aged, children and young persons, the physically disabled and mentally retarded, and juvenile delinquents. The ministry is also responsible for adoption, probation and rehabilitation.

Municipal social welfare departments are located in Jerusalem, Tel Aviv and Haifa and local offices are run in over 180 smaller settlements, including forty for Arab and Druze communities. Assistance is provided for basic needs, such as living expenses, rent and national insurance, and special needs, such as help for the chronically ill at home. In 1970–1, 74,500 families received regular or partial relief. In addition approximately 46,500 families received help through counselling or in some other way not involving direct financial aid. Adding to these the families who received help from voluntary bodies, it becomes clear that over half a million people or one-sixth of Israel's population relied on social welfare—an indication of the scale of Israel's problem.

HEALTH SERVICES

Israel inherited an effective and well-equipped health service; it had been pioneered by the Hadassah Medical Organisation (sponsored by the Women's Zionist Organisation of America) and the Histadrut, whose wide-ranging public health division, Kupat Holim, was—as it is now—the largest medical service in the country. During the period of the mandate, expertly staffed hospitals and a network of clinics provided for the needs of urban and rural Jews, whereas the health services of the mandatory government served mainly the non-Jewish population.

A Ministry of Health was created with the establishment of the state and it became the main administrative and co-ordinating authority on matters of national health. Kupat Holim, however, continued to provide the only comprehensive health insurance scheme with a membership embracing the majority of the population. Hadassah gradually transferred certain of its functions to the Ministry of Health, but it too continued to play a leading part in the health service, especially in the joint operation with the Hebrew University of the Hadassah University Hospital and in the maintenance of clinics and guidance centres for young people.

With the great influx of immigrants, Israel's health services soon proved inadequate. Not only were a large proportion of the newcomers ailing, they also brought diseases and health risks hitherto unknown, and it is estimated that 13 per cent suffered from chronic illnesses. Those from Asia and Africa were plagued with malaria and trachoma and had little understanding of basic hygiene. Furthermore, many who came from Europe remembered the ghettos and concentration camps and were in need of mental care. The major health services co-operated with the ministry to meet the urgent needs of immigration, and Israel was fortunate to possess a large quota of physicians and surgeons who had left Central and Eastern Europe in the course of the two previous decades. The success of the health service can be measured by the life expectancy of the population which is now higher than most Western countries. It averages 69·5 years for males and 73·2 for females, compared with 66·6 and 72·7 respectively in the United States and 67·3 and 72·4 in Britain. Israel has also demonstrated that the disease problems associated with the Middle East can be conquered with effective health and sanitation programmes. Tuberculosis is not as rampant as formerly; malaria has been eradicated and venereal diseases, though present, are a comparatively minor problem. The principal causes of death are diseases to the heart and circulatory system, malignant neoplasms, and diseases of early infancy, including malformations and pneumonia. The infant mortality rate which rose to 51·7 per 1,000 live births among Jews in 1949 has fallen steadily to 19·2 among Jews, but remains as 39·4 among Arabs. The incidence of infant diseases is also higher in Arab communities and Oriental Jewish populations.

In 1971, there were a total of 23,758 beds in 161 hospitals of all types, of which the government was responsible for 34 hospitals and 8,000 beds. Apart from the missions and private hospitals, Kupat Holim continues to play a major role in health services and maintains over 1,000 clinics, 9 general hospitals, 5 specialised hospitals, 15 convalescent homes, 147 laboratories and 233 pharmacies. The Hagem David Adom—Israel's equivalent of the Red Cross—runs first-aid stations, blood banks and ambulances with a staff of 6,000 volunteers. Malben is another voluntary organisation and is concerned mainly with aged and physically handicapped new immigrants. It maintains over forty old people's homes and a youth rehabilitation centre for mentally retarded immigrant children.

Despite Israel's claim to a welfare state, a free national health service has not been instituted, partly because of the pressure of the Histadrut which is unwilling to relinquish its Kupat Holim. As a health insurance fund, however, Kupat Holim relieves the anxiety of heavy medical expenses. These are covered by its members' dues which are proportionate to income, employers' payments and government grants. In 1971 the budget was IL500 (£49 or $118) million and the organisation had a combined membership of 2,090,000.

MATERNAL AND CHILD WELFARE

Israel has a countrywide network of mother-and-child health stations, maintained largely by the ministry, but also by Kupat Holim and other bodies. The first child welfare clinic was pioneered by Hadassah and opened in Jerusalem in 1921. By 1948 there were 120 such centres and these were transferred to the

Ministry of Health. Baby clinics and children's homes are also
maintained by the women's branch of the Zionist Organisation.

Full medical supervision through pregnancy and the post-
natal period is provided, but one major problem has been the
reluctance of immigrant expectant mothers to enter hospital for
child delivery. Hospital allowances, however, as part of the
national insurance scheme, have been effective in the steady decline of the mortality rate. Following delivery, systematic and
comprehensive post-natal care is provided, and a careful check
is kept on the child's physical, mental and social development.

Improvement in child health and welfare is most noticeable
among the Arab population. Arab women are becoming
increasingly less passive about the problems of pregnancy and
the size of families. In East Jerusalem the mother-and-child
health clinic, opened in 1968, now averages around 2,000
annual patients. Teaching programmes on child care are also
organised and advice is given on birth control, particularly to
Arab women who have given birth to genetically abnormal
children.

FOOD AND DRINK

Within the last decade Israel's food supply pattern has been
transformed from one of scarcity to one of relative abundance,
especially in respect to vegetables, fruit, milk and milk products. During the early years of statehood the low level of agricultural production and the increasing demands from
immigration produced severe food shortages, and price control
and rationing were introduced. Israel is not self-sufficient in
basic items such as wheat and sugar, but the share of local
agriculture in supplying home needs has steadily increased.
Malnutrition and vitamin deficiency are found in some rural
areas and among lower income groups in urban areas, but are
gradually becoming less evident.

In view of the variation in background and cultural characteristics of the population, only broad generalisations can be
made on the national diet. It can be said, however, that the

general pattern of food consumption is akin to that of Western Europe and the United States, although Israel has a higher intake of cereals, vegetables and fruit and a lower intake of red meat and sugar. Animal proteins are abundantly available in the form of milk and poultry products; in 1970, according to the International Egg Commission, the average Israeli consumed 412 eggs—a figure higher than that of any other country. The average intake of poultry meat was 65·6 lb—equivalent to 62 per cent of the meat diet. Popular vegetable items include potatoes, tomatoes, beans, onions, peppers, egg plants, carrots, cabbages, cucumbers, chick peas and lentils; these are complemented by a wide range of locally grown tropical, subtropical and temperate fruits. The Israeli prefers to buy food items fresh from the local markets.

The per capita consumption of cereals provides 43 per cent of the daily calorie intake and is eaten primarily as wheat flour in bread. The types of bread include the flat oriental style, *pitta*, or the Jewish *matzohs*, and dark and light European varieties, the latter increasing in popularity in recent years. Wheat is also used in *burghul*, parboiled wheat, chiefly by Oriental Jews. Small quantities of rye, oats and corn meal are consumed and rice is preferred to potatoes by Oriental Jews. Chick peas (*houmous*), another oriental staple, have now become universally popular in a dish called *felafel* consisting of chick-pea paste, fried in small cakes and served in a *pitta* roll with a dressing of oil and salad. This has become Israel's ubiquitous snack.

The main differences in diets rest primarily on a cultural basis rather than on the availability of produce. European Jews are the main meat and potato eaters, whereas Oriental Jews prefer rice, vegetables, salads and oily fried food. These broad categories cover a large number of variant groups and diets are as heterogeneous as national origins. Among the European Jews, for example, there are Hungarians who eat goulashes and prefer paprika seasoning; Czechs with their dumplings and *knoedl*; Americans and British with a preference for roast beef, steak and chops; Poles who like a meat and potato diet, and the Balkan groups preferring olives, tomato paste, dried fish, goat cheese and egg plant.

Equally varied are the oriental diets. Migrants from Tunisia

and Morocco eat *tagine*, a mixed stew of pulses, rice and potatoes with vegetables and oil. Semolina and pastes cooked with
honey and syrup are common desserts. Iraqi Jews combine vegetables with meat, fish or rice, and vine leaves, peppers or *lazi*
(sugarbeet leaves) are stuffed with rice and meat. The Arab
population has also preserved its own dietary habits. In rural
areas it depends chiefly on the crops grown in the local district.
Bedouins depend largely on their flocks, subsisting on a milk
diet supplemented by cereals and some dried fruit.

Of equal importance to the variety of ethnic groups with individual eating habits is the continued observance of ancient restrictions governing Jewish food. Prohibitions, originally
dictated by conditions of climate and hygiene and later incorporated into religious law, regulate the diet of a major part of
Israel's population and the food available in most of the hotels
and restaurants. *Kosher* cuisine follows the dietary rules laid
down in the Pentateuch and designates only cattle, sheep and
poultry as suitable meat for eating. Pork and bacon are forbid-
den and also shellfish. The regulations cover the slaughter of
animals and the preparation of carcasses; while a strict separa-
tion of meat and dairy produce at the table is mandatory, that
is, milk, butter and cheese may not be served before, with or

---

Much of Israel's housing, especially in the major cities is standardised
and aesthetically unpleasing. Private and municipal associations have
been formed to counteract the deterioration in appearance and facilities
in housing estates.

Outposts of individuality in housing development are largely confined to
private initiative. The famous Jerusalem stone provides greater opportunities for architectural experiment in house design.

after a meal containing any kind of meat. Taken in its strictest form, *kosher* law even requires that linen, crockery and utensils for a meal should be different from those used when eating dairy products.

It is impossible to predict whether a national Israeli diet will eventually emerge from these variant standards. *Kosher* cuisine probably comes nearest to the ideal, but there has been considerable cultural borrowing and many oriental recipes are now standard in the kitchens of European Jews.

A much more universal pattern is revealed in the country's drinking habits. The Israelis are a remarkably sober people and drunkenness is a rare phenomenon. If a problem of alcohol exists, it is that they do not buy enough. The government has sponsored propaganda programmes to encourage drinking and hence to support the local wine industry. To some extent this has paid off, but by far the most common drinks are mineral waters and a wide variety of fresh fruit and vegetable juices.

Constant experimentation has made Israel nearly self-sufficient in food produce and the *kibbutzim* have played a unique role in this progress. At Ashdot Yaacob, near Lake Kinneret, workers tend vines for the country's expanding wine and table grape market.

Large investments have been made in textile and garment manufacture and most factories are run on modern lines. At the Gibor factory stockings are examined before despatch.

5

How They Work

If 'ease is inimical to civilisation', as Toynbee claimed, then Israel vividly illustrates the creative interplay between challenge and response on a national level. The country has made spectacular progress in developing a modern economic structure in a land of limited potential. In spite of the continuous flow of immigrants and the absence of settled and peaceful relations with neighbouring states, both of which have left deep imprints on economic conditions and development, Israel has shown substantial achievements in practically every branch of production. From 1950 onwards, the rate of economic growth has been one of the highest in the world, with gross national product increasing more than fivefold. This is equivalent to an annual growth rate of over 9 per cent, compared with 3·3 per cent for the United States, 5 per cent for Denmark, 5·3 per cent for West Germany and 9·5 per cent for Japan. In 1966–7, however, Israel paid the price for this over-rapid growth with a fairly severe depression. Unemployment increased and immigration dropped and was replaced by emigration. But considerable economic recovery was evident before the 1967 June War and further disruption, as a result of the conflict, was offset by the influx of financial aid from abroad. The added burden of defence expenditure was covered by increases in direct and indirect taxation. The protracted nature of the Yom Kippur War, however, produced further financial problems for Israel and was one of the reasons for the devaluation of the Israeli lira in November 1974.

The dramatic changes in the country's livelihood since 1948 is often attributed to the initiative and ingenuity of the Israelis and their will to succeed. The establishment of the state changed significantly the scope and direction of Jewish development, and faced with economic dissociation from its neighbours Israel was forced to plan independently from the rest of its geographical region. During the early days of statehood there was much experimentation on a trial and error basis, but gradually a sound body of experience and original methods were developed to tackle the country's unique economic problems. Although such methods cannot be readily transplanted to other developing regions, Israel has extended widespread technical aid and guidance to countries in Africa, South America and South East Asia.

Israel's rapid economic expansion, it should be stressed, would not have been possible without massive financial support from abroad. This has amounted to several billion dollars, which have come in the form of private gifts and bond purchases, extensive grants and loans, chiefly from the United States, and reparations from West Germany in partial payment for Jewish losses during World War II. The latter, paid in accordance with the Hague agreement of 1952, were completed in March 1966, by which time West Germany had paid around £216 million. This foreign aid has fostered the building of an economic structure in many ways similar to that of the industrialised countries of the West. Whether Israel can become an economically viable state and continue at this desired economic standard when outside aid terminates remains to be seen. The Capital Investment Law was introduced to encourage the flow of private capital into the country and attractive benefits and concessions are offered to approved enterprises. The State of Israel bonds, introduced in 1951, have proved an important source of capital and have earned more than £750 ($1,750) million from their sale in Europe and the Americas. This revenue has been invested through the Development Bank into every sector of the economy.

AGRICULTURE

The acquisition and settlement of agricultural land by Jewish immigrants was one of the basic objectives of the Zionist movement in Palestine. The motives were ideological and political, for agricultural work, especially within collective and cooperative settlements, was regarded as the main means of fulfilling the Zionist and pioneering ideal of redeeming the ancestral homeland. With the establishment of the state the emphasis on agricultural expansion continued, but it was now related to the economic necessity of developing alternative food supplies previously imported from Arab countries or produced by Palestinian Arabs. Prior to 1948, three-quarters of the Palestinian Arabs were cultivators and produced most of the grain, meal, fodder and vegetable oil. The majority of the Jewish settlements concentrated on mixed farming and citrus production, but were forced, after 1948, to expand and diversify production to meet domestic requirements. The added problems of conserving foreign exchange and feeding a rapidly expanding immigrant population made an increase in agricultural output and the optimum use of resources imperative. Initially the difficulties appeared insurmountable. The majority of Jews had no farming background and those who did were strange to Mediterranean and semi-arid conditions. But the fact that the new farmers were novices made them extremely receptive to innovation and experiment. Improved methods, an increase in the farming skills of immigrants, and heavy investment in equipment, irrigation and crop research led to the desired increase in productivity and the area under cultivation. The latter rose from 400,000 acres in 1948–9 to 1,028,000 in 1971–2, of which 480,000 acres were irrigated. A turning point was reached in Israeli agriculture around 1964 when agricultural exports were more than enough to pay for the import of food items such as grain, meat, tea and coffee. In a US Department of Agriculture study of the performances of twenty-six developing countries published at the end of 1965, Israel's agricultural economy was judged to be the most successful; for this reason its methods and results have continued to arouse interest abroad. Today, agriculture is one of the most efficient branches of the economy and subject to strict government control through marketing boards, land and water allocation and subsidies. It is important to stress, however, that 94·5 per cent of the country's total agricultural output is produced by Jewish farmers and comes from some 850 settlements or villages. The Arab economy remains retarded in spite of efforts to narrow the gap between the two systems. Arab production has multiplied six times since 1948 but outmoded methods, land fragmentation and poor rotations are still the causes of inefficiency.

The significance of collective settlements in Israel's remarkable agricultural performance cannot be overemphasised. The *kibbutzim* have constituted the spearhead of the Jewish drive to land settlement and, together with the *moshavim*, continue to be in the forefront of agricultural expansion and innovation. In 1971, collective settlements accounted for roughly two-thirds of the Jewish farming population. Another cardinal factor in the rapid progress of agriculture is that nine-tenths of the farmland is publicly owned, either by the state or the Jewish National Fund. Land owned by the JNF is held in trust for the nation and let on forty-nine-year leases, a system that follows the principle of the biblical jubilee and relates to the religious motivations of the early Zionists. Similar general principles are observed in the administration of state lands. The National Land Authority represents the government, and the Land Development Authority represents the JNF in all matters of ownership, reclamation and afforestation. The JNF has reclaimed over 200,000 acres of land, opening up the Jezreel and Huleh valleys, the Jerusalem Corridor, and the northern Negev. Its work has contributed to Israel's security and strengthened the country's economic structure.

Publicly owned land provides the key to comprehensive land-settlement planning, of which the most advanced project is that of the Lachish area, in south-west Judaea, inaugurated in 1955. Others include the Ta'anach area, south-east of Afula (1956); the Adullam area in the Judaean Hills (1957); the Korazim area, north of Lake Kinneret (1962); and the Besor area to the south-west of Beersheba. Certain clashes have taken place between the government and national organisations, particularly with the Jewish Agency. According to a general agreement the JA is responsible for the settlement of new immigrants and the state looks after and regulates agricultural activities. This distinction is difficult to make and disagreements have taken place between the two bodies. The Agency directs immigrants to those branches of agriculture easiest to them, whereas the Ministry of Agriculture tries to encourage production in those branches whose development is most important from a national economic point of view.

A major key to Israel's successful agricultural progress has been the maximum utilisation of its meagre water resources. Rain falls mainly in winter, and the annual average drops rapidly from 40in in the north to 1in at Eilat. Thus large areas of the country have rainfall totals that fall below the minimum required for dry farming even when there is no drought. The basis of Israel's water planning involves the sharing of resources from the wetter north with the dry south, and Lake Kinneret, in particular, has been developed as the main reservoir for storage. The Negev soil is fertile, provided it is watered, and an extensive area in the north of over 375,000 acres is flat and suitable for mechanised cultivation. A major problem facing irrigation engineers is that water is found at low altitudes and has to be pumped to reach the higher farmland and agricultural settlements.

A special water administration is responsible for the control and regulation of both the supply and consumption of water, and large-scale projects have increased the irrigated area from 75,000 acres in 1948 to 480,000 acres in 1972. Both national and regional water schemes are interconnected to form an integrated countrywide distribution system; its basis is the National Water Carrier, a massive 9ft conduit directing water from the Jordan Valley southwards into Judaea and the Negev. It is linked with the Yarkon project which carries water in two pipelines from Rosh Ha'ayin near Tel Aviv to the northern Negev. Another major development is the Galilee-Kishon project which brings water to the fertile but under-watered Vale of Jezreel, where an artificial lake has been created on the Kishon river near Haifa.

When fully developed, the water resources—directly or indirectly interconnected by the national water grid—will have an annual capacity of about 1,600 million cubic metres. This figure represents almost all of Israel's proven water resources

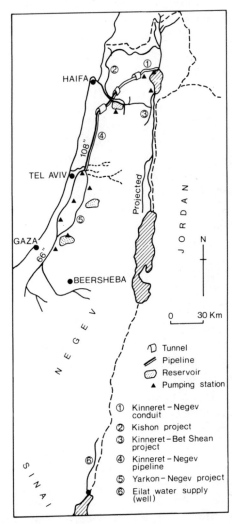

Water projects

and is sufficient to irrigate only 41 per cent of the country's irrigable land. Strict economy and efficient control over water-use are, therefore, necessary. Further methods and experiments, including the interception of storm water and the reclamation of waste water, are being developed accordingly.

Israel has also had considerable success in inducing rainfall by cloud-seeding and recent progress in the desalination of sea and brackish water may well prove a major alternative source for agricultural, industrial and domestic uses, once costs become acceptable. The experience gained in winning water under difficult conditions is being applied in other developing countries where Israeli specialists have been invited to advise.

Another aspect of Israel's successful agricultural expansion is the rigid policy of soil conservation. This is directed by the National Land Authority and the Soil Conservation Division of the Ministry of Agriculture. Contour ploughing on steep slopes, to prevent soil erosion, is obligatory by law, and protective channels have been dug to divert run-off from heavy rains and to regulate water flow in the wet season. Israel's conservation philosophy is simple: what has been won from nature with difficulty cannot be allowed to revert to the wild by irresponsible farming methods.

PRINCIPAL AGRICULTURAL PRODUCTS

The combined results of reclamation, irrigation and conservation, together with scientific methods of production, now mean that Israeli agriculture is one of the most efficient branches of the economy. It has been transformed from an extensive and mainly dry-farming system into an intensive and modern irrigated husbandry. Diversification and increased productivity has meant that the country is now self-sufficient in vegetables and dairy produce, though large imports of meat and cereals are still necessary. Agricultural policy is no longer dominated by the demands of mass immigration and there has been a shift of emphasis from food crops to industrial crops, such as cotton, sugarbeet and groundnuts, and to crops which can directly or indirectly earn foreign currency—a wide range of fruits and vegetables and, more recently, flowers.

In 1971, 93,000 were employed in agriculture (and fishing), representing only 9·5 per cent of the total labour force. On the other hand, the export of agricultural products, including those of the food industry, constituted 24·7 per cent of the total value of exports. This, in itself, is a mark of the efficiency and high degree of scientific management of Israeli agriculture.

Fruit crops

The most important agricultural export and a mainstay of the Israeli economy is citrus fruit. It accounts for 20 per cent of agricultural produce, 20 per cent of total exports and 75 per cent of agricultural exports. The climate and soil of the coastal plain, particularly Sharon, are eminently suitable for the cultivation of citrus, provided irrigation is available, though recently plantations have been extended to Galilee and the Jordan and Jezreel valleys. The main variety of orange is the famous Shamouti (the 'Jaffa'), but other varieties are grown, together with grapefruit, lemons, tangerines and citrons, which spread the citrus season from mid-November to mid-May. The entire process of production is under the surveillance of the Citrus Control and Marketing Board which also concludes agreements with shipping companies, purchases insecticides, equipment and packing materials, and supervises the harvesting. In 1970–1, citrus output was 1,490,100 tons (compared with 272,000 in 1948–9) and earned £40 ($115) million in export proceeds. The chief markets are Britain, West Germany, Sweden, Switzerland, Finland and Austria. There is also a large home market and in 1970–1 over 520,000 tons went to the canning industry which supplies domestic demand and contributes substantially to the export market.

Most deciduous and tropical fruits are successfully grown in Israel. The grape is of particular importance; production (60,700 tons in 1970) is sufficient to supply the wine industry and the home market, leaving a surplus for export. The production of bananas (61,150 tons) has also steadily increased and exports continue to grow. Melons, plums, apricots, apples and pears are other important crops, together with strawberries, of which about 100 tons were exported in 1970. The production costs of most deciduous fruits are too high to make them competitive on the export market.

Industrial crops

Cotton was first introduced in 1953 and 35,300 tons of cotton lint was produced in 1970, together with 55,000 tons of cotton-seed. This now supplies the local demand from spinning mills built in development regions largely to employ immigrant labour. Similar crop and factory schemes for groundnuts (18,700 tons) and sugarbeet (237,000 tons) have been equally successful. Sugar cane, formerly cultivated on an experimental basis, was found to be unprofitable. Factories at Kiryat Gat and Afula, in the growing districts, refine the local beet produce as well as imported sugar.

Other crops

Israel is more or less self-sufficient in potatoes and a wide variety of vegetables, much of which are exported. Other old-established crops include olives and tobacco, while the most successful of the experimental crops are flax, sisal, sunflower and other oilseeds. Overseas demand for avocado pears and flowers has caused a steady rise in the areas under these crops, and they help to pay for those agricultural items which Israel still has to import. The area under wheat and barley, for example, is being steadily extended, but the country imports large quantities of cereals for breadmaking, although hard wheat for macaroni is exported to Italy. Greater progress has been made in the production of green fodder and hay, but substantial imports of animal feed are still required.

LIVESTOCK AND DAIRY PRODUCE

Considerable investment in research and development has been made to improve the country's livestock. Until recently cattle were raised mainly for dairy purposes, but surpluses of milk, self-sufficiency in butter and cheese, and continued emphasis by the government to reduce beef imports have led to an increasing concentration on cattle for meat. Experiments have been conducted to increase the grazing area for cattle, particularly in Galilee where afforestation areas are used, the livestock assisting with the control of weeds in plantations. In 1970,

35,600 tons of beef were produced for the home market; the current development plan calls for doubling the number of beef cows by 1975–6 to 29,000 head. In 1970, Israel produced 487,000 kilolitres of milk and the yearly average yield per cow is among the highest in the world.

Most table meat is still provided by poultry (101,700 tons in 1970). Poultry raising has long been one of the basic branches of farming and was of particular importance for the absorption of new immigrants as it demands little farming experience. The government guarantees minimum prices for poultry meat and also controls the producer and consumer prices for eggs. In 1970, the production of table eggs totalled 94·8 million dozen and exports of edible, hatching and frozen eggs are increasing.

The sheep population has also expanded considerably since 1948 and experiments have been made to develop cross-breeds suitable for wool and mutton. At present, sheep are mainly bred for milk used in cheese products. Both Arab and Jewish farmers keep goats for milk and hides, but owing to the damage they inflict on pastures and forests efforts are being made to persuade farmers to switch to sheep and cattle raising.

A sideline in Israeli farming is the breeding of mink, chinchillas and other fur animals. This helps to support some hill settlements and is connected with the country's fashion industry.

FORESTRY

Afforestation plays a special role in all development projects for economic reasons as well as for its value in landscaping and recreation. For centuries Palestine was denuded of the woods and forests for which it was famous in biblical and Roman times; only a few pockets remained in inaccessible regions, such as Mount Carmel, and in places in Upper Galilee. Most areas deteriorated into Mediterranean scrub of the maquis or garrigue type. The planting of trees had a strong emotional appeal for immigrants, especially those from northern countries where forests are an integral part of the landscape. The mandatory government had a strong bias towards afforestation and 12,000 acres of trees, chiefly pine, were planted during the British period in Judaea, Samaria and Lower Galilee. The JNF also set up a special system of donations for trees at every family and national occasion, and this became popular among Jews all over the world. After 1948, afforestation activities were speeded up as it provided employment and became a means of opening up mountainous regions. Plantations of pine, cypress and eucalyptus were also beneficial in preventing soil erosion and run-off.

Many woods and forests have been planted as national or personal memorials: some 60 million trees, for example, have been planted to commemorate the Jews destroyed by Nazism in Europe. There are also planting centres for tourists organised by the JNF. Well over 15 million saplings, or 60,000 acres, have been planted since 1948 and are now flourishing. A further 200,000 acres are earmarked for forestry development.

FISHERIES

Israel's fish supplies are derived from three main sources: sea fishing (trawling, inshore and deep-sea fishing), Lake Kinneret and fish-breeding ponds. Sea fishing has greatly expanded and Israeli fleets operate from the Canary Islands to the Indian Ocean and also off the South African Cape. Breeding in fish ponds, a special feature of the country, is handled mainly by *kibbutzim* and accounts for 60 per cent of the catch, which in 1970 amounted to 21,800 tons. Carp is the main type of fish bred and responds to a heavy demand, as it is the traditional fish diet of Eastern European Jews. The fish ponds are developed in areas where large quantities of water are available at low cost. These conditions are found along the Jordan Valley (Huleh, Kinrot at Bet She'an valleys) and in some stretches of the coastal plain. Four crops of fish are obtained each year; they are transported to the markets fresh in tanks. Scarcity of water has impeded further development of fish ponds, but there are plans to establish them in reservoir lakes constructed in connection with the national water project.

ENERGY AND NATURAL RESOURCES

Most of Israel's mineral resources are in the Negev, and have been discovered through extensive geological surveys since the achievement of independence. The most valuable minerals are phosphate, potash, common salt, bromide and sulphur, but in addition prospecting has discovered commercially workable deposits of copper, manganese, feldspar, bitumen-bearing rock and gypsum. The main extracting centres of the Negev are Sodom, Arad, Oron, Mitzpeh Ramon and Timna, and large public concerns have been established to exploit and process these raw materials. They include the Dead Sea Works at Sodom, Israel Chemicals and Phosphates (Oron), the Timna Copper Mines, Negev Ceramic Minerals and Arad Chemical Industries. To cope with the problems of transporting the output, which earns around £22 ($50) million in exports, a government-owned heavy trucking company was created, and the railway is being progressively extended into the Negev to provide an eventual link between the Dead Sea and Eilat and the Mediterranean ports of Ashdod and Haifa (see Chapter 6).

Israel has no coal and both the topography and rainfall regime are unsuited to the development of hydro-electric power. Oil was discovered for the first time in 1955 at Heletz and Kochav, near Ashkelon, and natural gas from Rosh Zohar near the Dead Sea is piped to the Sodom works. In 1970, thirty-four wells produced 83,000 tons of oil, but this covers only a minor proportion of Israel's needs and further prospecting is being carried out by foreign and local companies. Initial results of offshore tests for oil in the Mediterranean are encouraging and Israel's potential oil reserves are estimated at between 70 and 300 million tons. At present large imports of oil from the Persian Gulf reach Eilat and are pumped north to the refineries at Haifa, but it is hoped that enough oil and natural gas will be found within the next five years to supply the country's needs. The Petroleum Law (1952) regulates prospecting and exploitation, ensures state royalties on a reasonable scale (12·5 per cent), and provides sufficient inducement for the investor and speculator.

With a scarcity of natural power resources, the expansion of electricity supply is crucial for the development of the economy. Energy to industry is based entirely on electricity, generated by thermic plants using oil fuel. The Israel Electric Corporation is government-owned and supervised by the Ministry of Development. Between 1948 and 1971, power station capacity increased eighteenfold to over 1·2 million kilowatts and total consumption rose from 246 million kilowatts to 5,852 million kilowatts. The national grid is based on three main plant concentrations at Tel Aviv, Ashdod and Haifa, with an auxiliary plant at Jerusalem.

The dependence upon imported oil stresses the need for research into other sources of energy. The utilisation of solar energy on a large scale is still in the experimental stage, but for household requirements it is already used in the form of water heaters, and almost all newly built houses, especially on the coastal plain, have rooftop mirrors for solar heating. Most important, however, are the attempts to develop nuclear power. The state has its own Atomic Energy Commission composed of leading scientists, economists and administrators, and some research projects are carried out in co-operation with the International Atomic Energy Agency, Euratom and other institutions abroad. Provided nuclear power can be produced at competitive cost, the great advantage to Israel would be the long-term possibility of fuel storage.

MANUFACTURING INDUSTRY

The development of industry, like that of the economy as a whole, has been rapid, and today Israel produces a volume and variety of manufactured goods undreamed of in 1948. Between 1948 and 1971 output more than quintupled, growing by over 10 per cent a year and reaching £1,300 ($3,000) million in 1971. Industrial exports rose from £8 ($18) million to £260 ($600) million—an increase of 20 per cent a year; employment went up from 89,200 to 216,000, and output per worker, on average, by 4 per cent a year. This growth was achieved despite a number of limitations: a scarcity of raw materials and energy sources, a restricted local market and distance from export markets, and the political situation and the Arab boycott which keeps the majority of Middle Eastern countries closed to Israeli goods.

When the state was founded, output from industries set up during the mandatory regime was largely of consumer goods for local use, and of goods imported in a partly finished condition for final processing. The need for self-sufficiency in manufactured products and the necessity to create employment for a rapidly growing population turned Israel into the most industrially-minded country in the Middle East, and no efforts have been spared to speed and spread industrial expansion and diversification. Industries based on local agricultural products account for some 14 per cent of manufactures and employ around 38,000 persons. The food and beverage branches are highly diversified and widely dispersed over the country; 90 per cent of output is sold on the local market, but items such as juices, preserves, edible oil and canned groundnuts are exported. Wine production began at Rishon-le-Zion in 1890 and may be regarded as the oldest established Jewish enterprise in Israel. Domestic consumption has expanded with the growth of population, and exports of wine to America and Europe are increasing in importance. Tobacco and cigarette factories cater almost exclusively for the local market, blending home-grown varieties with imported leaf.

The textile and clothing industry, a field in which the Jews have a long-standing tradition, accounted for 15 per cent of total manufactures in 1971 and employed 53,000. The initial concentration of textiles was in the Tel Aviv and Haifa areas, but large factories have been introduced into development towns where they are often the principal basis for employment. Initially founded on the import of raw materials and semi-finished products, the industry now relies on Israeli-grown cotton, but also manufactures rayon, nylon, woollens and worsteds. The indifferent needs of the immigrant population has been replaced by the production of high-class goods which supply some of the most affluent world markets. Articles such as knitted apparel, raincoats and stockings earned £42 ($96) million on the export market in 1971.

Chemicals and petroleum products cover about 10 per cent

of industrial output, with 10,100 employees and annual exports of £23 ($53) million. A wide variety of pharmaceutical goods, drugs and medicines are produced, but the most important side of the chemical industry is the production of fertilisers based on local potash and other raw materials. A range of petroleum by-products are associated with the Haifa refineries.

Collectively, the metal branch of manufacturing employs the largest number of workers, though firms range from the largest factories in the country to one-man workshops. Basic production stages (steel rolling and casting) are concentrated in the Haifa Bay area and the metal is used for machinery, tool-making, household goods and transport equipment. Substantial progress has been made in the car industry (Haifa, Ashdod and Nazareth), which began with the assembly of parts, but is gradually proceeding to the production of its own models. A similar trend is noticeable in aircraft and shipbuilding. Israel Aircraft Industries at Lod is now the largest single industrial enterprise, employing over 13,500, and has produced the first wholly Israel-designed aircraft—the Arava and the Commodore Jet—as well as the Gabriel strike missile.

The cutting and polishing of diamonds is undoubtedly Israel's most important industry and in terms of the value of net

---

The Carmel Market adds a note of oriental disorganisation to Tel Aviv's otherwise impersonal streets. Its shops, carts and itinerant peddlers offer an inexhaustible range of goods and trading is conducted in an equally bewildering number of languages.

Dizengoff Street is Tel Aviv's social centre and intellectual forum. Lined by some of the city's most popular shops and cafés, people converge here day and night to see and be seen.

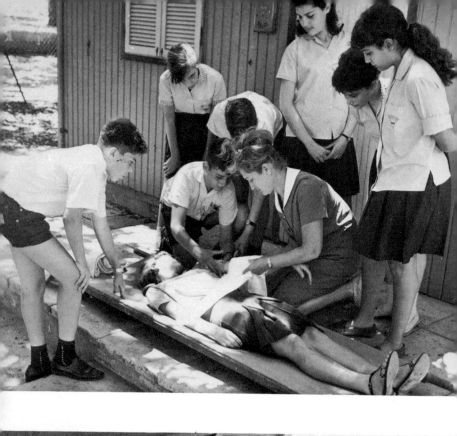

exports—£88 ($203) million in 1971—it vies with citrus. There
are over 400 plants engaged in the industry, providing employment for nearly 11,000 people. The first plant was opened at
Netanya, but the main concentration today is in the Tel Aviv
conurbation where the Israel Diamond Exchange and Bourse
at Ramat Gan is the world's largest centre for the industry.
Negligible transport costs have led to the establishment of diamond plants in hill regions and development towns. Israel's
share of international trade in polished diamonds has risen
from 30 per cent to 80 per cent in medium-size stones, in which
the country specialises. Israel is thus second only to Belgium as
an international diamond centre.

Other industries are many and varied. The heavy consumption of cement by the building industry has been met from local
resources in recent years, leaving a surplus for export. The tyre
industry also meets local needs and exports to some twenty-five
different markets throughout the world.

THE TOURIST INDUSTRY

Tourism is a main source of foreign currency earnings and a
prominent productive branch in the economy. In 1971, over

Practical as well as academic instruction forms part of the school curricula. Pupils of an elementary school in Tel Aviv are taught the basic
methods of first aid.

The Tel Aviv–Haifa line offers a fast and frequent service between the
two cities. Engines are diesel and rolling-stock is modern, although
coaches are not heated in winter.

650,000 tourists visited the country, spending £66 ($155) million. Some 40 per cent came from the United States and 39 per cent from Europe.

Pilgrimage to the Holy Land was practised long before tourism developed as a modern and highly organised industry, but immediately following the establishment of the state the number of visitors increased annually, although there were interruptions as a result of political incidents. The Six Day War, in particular, disrupted previous trends, but in 1968 the 432,000 tourists represented a 48 per cent increase on the 1966 figure. The reunification of Jerusalem and the concentration of all its Holy Places within Israel, as well as unrestricted access to the administered areas, accounted for the increase.

As a holiday playground Israel, with its sunny climate, good beaches and varied scenery, compares favourably with other Mediterranean countries. Its main advantage in the tourist field, however, is the spiritual appeal of a country that contains a large number of Holy Places of three great religions. Israel's natural and cultural attractions have promoted a rapid expansion in hotel accommodation, transport and entertainment facilities, such developments being sponsored and supervised by the Ministry of Tourism. Information centres have been established in all towns and resort areas, and twenty tourist offices are operated in major cities abroad.

LABOUR AND WORKING CONDITIONS

Workers enjoy the full protection of the state and all matters concerning the labour force are the responsibility of the Ministry of Labour. By law, every person seeking employment, except in the professions or in work requiring special qualifications, must register at the government labour exchanges, of which there are fifteen regional centres with 164 branches and sections, including those for Arabs and young people aged fourteen to eighteen. Special exchanges for professional people exist in Tel Aviv, Jerusalem, Haifa and Beersheba.

Labour legislation lays down minimum standards of health, safety and working conditions; in 1951 the normal working day was limited to eight hours and the working week to forty-seven

hours. Thirty-six hours of continuous rest per week is mandatory, together with an annual holiday with pay of between fourteen and twenty-eight days, depending on position and
seniority. In 1953 and 1954 respectively, legislation was passed
governing the employment of women and children. Children
under fourteen may not be employed, and young workers of
fourteen to eighteen years receive a medical examination and
are prohibited or restricted from entering certain employment.
They have shorter working hours and night work is illegal.

Israeli women are among the most emancipated in the world
and play a vital role in the life of the country, not merely in its
economy but also in its defence, policing and government. The
Employment of Women Law prohibits certain types of employment and night work, but restrictions and prejudices are few;
all professions are open to women, who may become doctors,
journalists, advocates or engineers. Equal remuneration for the
same work applies to both private and state employment. Such
emancipation is not as common among the Arab sections of the
population, but the changing role of the Arab woman is demonstrated in East Jerusalem, where, since 1967, many have
acquired jobs through labour exchanges and are now paying
members of trade union organisations. The 'feminine' aspect
of women in employment is revealed chiefly in their entitle-
ment to twelve weeks' maternity leave with pay and several
months without pay!

Wages and working conditions are regulated by free negotiations between employers and the trade unions. The chief
labour relations officer of the Ministry of Labour arbitrates in
disputes on his own initiative or at the request of either party,
and regional and central tribunals deal with alleged breaches
of labour laws or violation of agreements. Strikes are permitted
and it is interesting that, although there is a low incidence of
industrial walk-outs, the number of strikes in services and professional employment is high.

TRADE UNIONISM

The Israel labour movement goes back more than seventy
years, to the time of the early Zionists who attempted to estab-

lish a self-supporting national society in Palestine. It was not until 1920 however, that the labour movement developed into a national organisation which gave birth to the Histadrut—the General Federation of Labour in Israel. This is the largest voluntary body in the country and as well as trade union work it engages in economic development, social insurance, education and cultural activities. Membership is open to all workers, including those belonging to co-operatives and the liberal professions, and dues amounting to 4·5–7 per cent of wages pay for all trade union services and health and social benefits.

In 1971, the Histadrut had an adult membership of 1,240,000; in addition, over 100,000 young people under eighteen years of age belonged to its direct affiliate—the Organisation of Working and Student Youth. The main religious labour organisations, Hapoel Hamizrahi and Poalei Agudat Israel, also belong to the Histadrut trade union and welfare service sections. These religious organisations have a collective membership of over 130,000 which means that, in total, the Histadrut covers some 90 per cent of all Israeli workers and their families. The other important religious labour organisation is the Histadrut Ha'ovdim Haleumit (the National Labour Federation) which was founded in 1934. It has 80,000 members and runs its own insurance, health and welfare schemes.

All members take part in the Histadrut elections which appoint the General Council and the Executive Committee. The latter elects the Executive Bureau which is responsible for day-to-day policy. All trade union affairs are organised through elected works committees, local labour councils and thirty-eight national unions covering most occupations and trades. The entire general body is affiliated to the International Confederation of Free Trade Unions and is active in the International Labour Movement and the International Co-operative Alliance.

It is paradoxical that Israel's major trade union is also the country's largest single employer of labour. Thus collective agreement and wage bargaining is often directed against itself. The reason for this is historical. During the mandate the Histadrut regarded one of its main tasks as the provision of work for the unemployed. This was achieved through organising productive co-operatives and small construction groups, which quickly developed into large contracting and industrial enterprises. The biggest is Solel Boneh, a building and public works company with over 30,000 employees. Others include Hamashbir Hamerkazi (Cooperative Wholesale Society) which supplies agricultural settlements and urban consumers' co-operatives, and Tnuva, an agricultural marketing co-operative which handles over two-thirds of all farm produce. The Histadrut also controls, wholly or partly, the bus co-operatives, the Workers' Bank, insurance and credit institutions, and has powerful interests in shipping companies.

WAGES AND INCOME TAX

The Histadrut is the major institution influencing the level of wages. Wages consist of four components—a basic wage, a cost of living allowance, special allowances (eg family allowances) and fringe benefits, including severance pay, paid holidays, sickness and maternity leave, social and medical insurance and pension funds. The cost of living allowance was introduced during World War II to prevent inflation from decreasing real wages. Many changes have been introduced into the system over the years, but it has maintained its basic characteristics. If the consumer price index rises beyond a predetermined amount during a given period, employees are given an automatic increase in basic wages, equal in percentage to the rise in prices. Israel's cost of living, it should be stressed, has risen through most of the period since the state was established. The cost of living index for October 1971 stood at 123·6 against 111·3 for the same month a year earlier (1969 = 100).

Real wages are also reduced by the country's heavy system of taxation. Income tax is levied on earned and unearned income, whether it originates in Israel or is received abroad. PAYE is in operation and the employer deducts tax on emoluments from weekly or monthly wages, salaries and pensions as they are paid. The usual types of relief are granted, but tax rates are steeply graded from 22·5 to 62·5 per cent on progressive portions of taxable income. An additional Defence Levy of 15 per cent was charged on the tax payable in 1971, as well as a compulsory defence loan of 7 per cent on taxable income and a compulsory savings loan ranging from 1·1 to 3·2 per cent on total gross salary. These measures make the Israeli citizen the most highly taxed in the world.

Income tax on companies is equally heavy. In 1971, they paid a company profit tax of 35 per cent and a Defence Levy of 3 per cent. On the balance of the assessable profits after these deductions, income tax is also payable at 25 per cent, making an effective rate of 53·5 per cent.

6

How They Get About

DEVELOPMENT OF THE ROAD SYSTEM

Throughout much of its history the geographical position of Palestine has favoured its role as a communications link between Asia and Africa. The transit trade which crossed the country from Egypt to Asia Minor and Syria, and from the Mediterranean to the Red Sea was a valuable source of wealth. A number of immemorial routes pass through or near to Palestine and from earliest history to modern times they have formed the backbone of the region's communications system. The coastal road (the Via Maris or 'Way of the Sea' of the Romans) entered Palestine from Sinai and Egypt and followed the Mediterranean coastal plain northwards to Mount Carmel. At Megiddo it divided into several branches with important routes leading to Acre and Tyre and to Damascus. To the east of the Jordan valley the King's Road followed the Transjordan Plateau and connected Arabia with Damascus. These major caravan routes were augmented by a third north-south axis which was of regional rather than international significance. For the most part it followed the Judaean and Samarian uplands and linked Beersheba, Hebron, Jerusalem and Shechem (Nablus) with Megiddo and then with Acre and highland Galilee.

Generally speaking, east-west connections were less important, mainly because of topographic difficulties, and only three transverse connections fulfilled major functions in the basic route network. One led from Jaffa to Jerusalem and then Jericho, another from Megiddo to the Jordan crossing near Ubeidiya and a third from Hefer through Shechem to the Jordan at Adam (today's Damiya Bridge). These east-west routes were

99

responsible for the economic significance of a number of coastal towns and for the strategic importance of inland centres, such as Jerusalem, Shechem and Megiddo. The latter, in particular, dominated the whole movement of trade in northern Palestine.

Successive administrators perpetuated and added to these early route alignments and the Romans had a lasting effect on communications. The first route to be paved was the Via Maris and, after the Jewish revolt of AD 66–70, the basic network was extended into a complex system which facilitated the movement of troops and the expansion of international commerce. Among the important Roman-built highways were the routes Caesarea-Antipatras-Jerusalem, Gaza-Jerusalem, Jerusalem-Megiddo and Acre-Tiberias. A large number of highways were also constructed in areas of difficult topography, particularly in the Negev.

The elaborate network fell into disrepair with the end of Roman rule, but was somewhat revived during the short-lived Crusader interlude when the Mediterranean was reopened to international trade. By the nineteenth century, the roads had decayed into tortuous paths and goods were transported on camels and donkeys. Tourists and pilgrims to the Holy Places in Judaea and Galilee complained of the lack of wheeled transport and of the discomforts of the traditional pack animals. Towards the end of the century the growing streams of pilgrims made road improvement inevitable and priority was given to the routes to the sacred cities—for example, the links between Jaffa and Jerusalem, Haifa and Nazareth and the lengthwise route from Hebron, through Bethlehem, Jerusalem and Nablus, to Nazareth. But, by 1914, it was reported that only the Jaffa–Jerusalem road was in fair order and towns such as Safad and Nablus could be reached only by animal or on foot.

The repair, improvement and extension of the road system, primarily for strategic purposes, was a prime objective of the mandatory administration and it was based on two main axes. The Haifa to Beersheba road via the towns of Afula, Jenin, Nablus, Jerusalem and Hebron remained the chief highway until 1937, but was complemented by a coastal road from Haifa through Hadera, Petah Tiqwa, Ramla and Gaza, to Beersheba. The two arteries were linked by transverse routes

(Hadera–Afula, Netanya–Nablus, Jaffa–Jerusalem), but the network totally disregarded the needs of Jewish settlement and not until World War II was a direct road link constructed between Tel Aviv and Haifa. The partition of Palestine in 1948 necessitated a complete reorientation of communications. In particular, the east-west routes from the coast to the Jordan valley lost their former significance and the artificiality of political boundaries meant that even local roads had to be re-routed. The Jordanian West Bank territory created serious communication problems for Israel, and roads from Jerusalem to Beersheba and to Haifa and Galilee were forced to follow circuitous paths. An immediate step following the acquisition of West Bank Jordan in 1967 was the improvement of the hill routes from Jerusalem to Beersheba, via Hebron, and from Jerusalem to Haifa and Galilee, via the Samarian towns of Ramallah, Nablus and Jenin.

Modern road improvements

In spite of the difficulties caused by political fragmentation, Israel's small areal extent has greatly aided the development of an efficient road network. Since the establishment of the state, road improvements and extensions have been given top priority and have been a decisive factor in the country's economic progress. Agriculture depends on roads for its supplies and the marketing of its products; likewise industry and the defence forces depend on well-surfaced highways with good feeder roads. In 1972 there were almost 5,800 miles of first-class roads, 2,600 miles of which were maintained by the government and local authorities, 3,000 miles by local authorities alone, and the small remainder by private bodies. The principal traffic arteries connect the three main cities of Tel Aviv, Jerusalem and Haifa, and large sums of money have been invested in their widening and realignment, to keep pace with economic expansion and the rapid annual increase in private and commercial vehicles.

The four-lane Tel Aviv–Haifa highway carries the heaviest road traffic. It is largely coastal and was constructed in the early 1950s via the towns of Herzliya, Netanya and Hadera.

From Haifa it continues northwards to Acre, Nahariya and the settlements near the Lebanese border. The parallel road to the east of the new highway was, prior to 1967, the only road

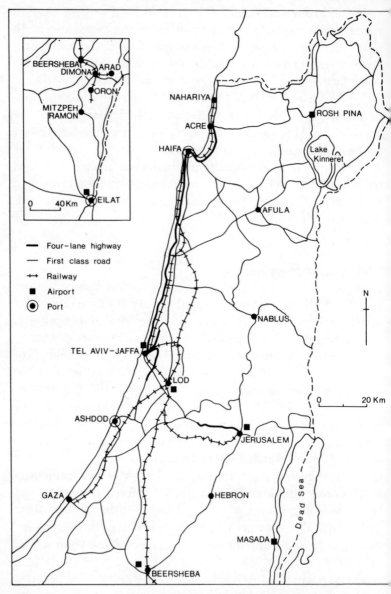

Communications infrastructure

connection between Jerusalem and Haifa. At Hadera an important road via Afula connects with Nazareth and Tiberias, with extensions into northern Galilee and Golan. South of Tel Aviv the coastal road to Ashdod, Ashkelon and Gaza is being transformed into a four-lane highway, as is the route between Jerusalem and Tel Aviv.

Undoubtedly the greatest strides in roadbuilding have been made in the Negev where the main highways connect 'settled' Israel with Beersheba, Dimona, Arad, Sodom and Eilat. At the forefront of this network is the implementation of a national road link between Eilat and Haifa—a 'dry Suez Canal' which will facilitate the rapid exchange of goods between the two ports. Planners have also discussed a super-highway across the Sinai Peninsula which would terminate at Sharm el Sheikh on the Red Sea.

TRAFFIC AND PUBLIC TRANSPORT

Israel is overwhelmingly a country of road users and the growth of motorised vehicles since 1948 has been spectacular. In 1972 the number of privately owned cars was over 197,000; in addition, there were over 79,000 trucks and trailers, 39,000 motor cycles and scooters, 4,900 buses and 3,700 taxis. It has been calculated that there is one vehicle for every fourteen Israelis and forty-seven vehicles to every kilometre of highway. Traffic congestion is acute in and around the major cities and Tel Aviv, in particular, suffers from imminent traffic paralysis. The great increase in private cars (estimated at 15,000 per annum) and the conurbation's high bus density are largely responsible. Driving in Tel Aviv is adventurous and no sedative for the nerves. Traffic keeps to the right, but hand signals and road manners are as varied as the drivers' countries of origin. Official tests, both for driving and road worthiness, are enforced by the government and a number of driving schools are under state control. The police are also vigilant in detecting, and the courts in punishing, offenders and road safety campaigns and accident prevention organisations have been effective in diminishing the number of fatal casualties. In order to ease traffic congestion a feasibility study has been made on the possibility of building a rapid transit line, partly underground, in the Tel Aviv area. With the exception of the two kilo-metre-long funicular railway in Haifa, Israeli cities have no urban rail systems.

Buses are the chief means of public transport and the undis-puted masters of the roads. It is possible to travel the entire length of the country on scheduled routes; this has been a decisive factor in breaking down isolation in frontier areas and in opening up developing regions. Immediately following the territorial successes of the 1967 war Israeli buses comple-mented the Arab vehicles in the administered zones and tours were operated from West Jerusalem to the scenic and historic attractions of the West Bank, Sinai and Golan.

The Egged Company, with a fleet of around 2,500 vehicles, represents one of the largest bus companies in the world, sur-passed only by Greyhound in the US and by London Trans-port. It operates on both inter-urban and urban routes, except in Tel Aviv, where the city and suburbs are served by the Dan Company. Private transport is not prohibited on the Sabbath, but most buses, except in the Arab areas, stop running after 5 pm on Fridays. This regulation is left to the discretion of the municipal authorities and in Haifa there is no curtailment. This is partly a reflection of the progressive down-to-earth atti-tude of Haifa's municipal council, but a more practical reason is the location of the city's residential areas on the steep slopes of Mount Carmel!

Taxis are almost as common as buses on Israeli roads. The regular taxi ('special') is metered, and similar to its counter-parts in Europe and America, but the service (*sherut*) taxi is Israel's patent. *Sheruts* are a hold-over from the early years of statehood when public transport was in short supply and in many ways they remain Israel's most convenient form of travel. Basically, the *sheruts* are large, not necessarily new, cars refitted to carry up to seven passengers. They operate between the larger city centres and between almost all sizeable towns on fixed schedules and routes. On some popular runs *sheruts* may be hailed from the kerbside, but they tend to operate from fixed addresses which vary according to the destinations involved.

Sheruts do a flourishing business late at night and on Friday evenings and Saturdays when other forms of public transport are in short supply. Fares are 10–30 per cent higher than those of buses, but are fixed by law.

RAIL

In spite of the fact that rail travel is the cheapest form of transportation in Israel, the railways are secondary to the roads which carry the bulk of goods and passenger traffic. Railways account for under 5 per cent of all public transport passengers and collect around 2 per cent of passenger fares. The reasons for their relative unimportance are largely historical. Prior to independence the Jewish community relied mainly on motor transport, and strong workers co-operatives were developed for the conveyance of goods and passengers. Railways served, almost exclusively, the Arab areas and the fact that stations were located on the outskirts of towns, necessitating motor transport for access, again increased the dominance of the road. Today, however, a great deal of attention is being paid to the restoration and development of rail transport, with the double object of providing relief to the overburdened roads and of making possible the more economic carriage of bulky raw materials from the Negev to the ports of shipment.

Palestine's first railway was a narrow-gauge line which ran from Jaffa to Jerusalem. It was constructed in 1892 by a French concessionary company and served mainly the pilgrim and tourist traffic. In 1914 the Turks built the special-gauge Hejaz railway connecting Damascus with Medina through Amman, with a branch via Zemah and Afula to Haifa and a spur to Acre. During World War I the line was extended southward from Afula to Tulkarm and a further extension via Beersheba reached Quseima in 1916. Also during the war the British built the standard-gauge Sinai railway from El Qantara on the Suez Canal to Gaza, Lod and Haifa; in 1941 this was extended from Haifa to Beirut linking up with the Syrian and Anatolian networks. At the end of the mandate there were 470 kilometres of railways in Palestine, but the partition of the country meant that only a few sections of the system, amounting to less than a quarter, remained in Israeli hands. Many of the bridges and culverts, together with much of the track, were badly damaged and there was no rail communication between the three principal cities. An added problem was that, out of 7,000 railway employees who worked under the mandatory regime, there were only some 400 Jews remaining available for the new government, and the majority of these were clerks and fitters with little practical knowledge of running railways.

Work on the reconstruction of the network began immediately, and before the end of 1949 a train reached Jerusalem from Tel Aviv. The Haifa–Tel Aviv and Haifa–Jerusalem lines were reopened in spite of the difficulties caused by the necessity of bypassing Arab territory, and extensions to the network were made in the south. In 1972 the railway network consisted of 760 kilometres of standard-gauge track extending from Nahariya in the north to Oron in the Negev. The line of first importance, completed in 1952, connects Tel Aviv with Haifa, via Netanya and Hadera and is closely followed by the line from Tel Aviv to Kiryat-Gat and Beersheba (1956). The extension of the system into the Negev was planned for the carriage of raw materials rather than passengers; the railway reached Dimona in 1965 and the phosphate works at Oron in 1970, with a spur to Tzela, near Arad. Ultimately it is planned to reach the port of Eilat. The bulk of the freight traffic consists of grain, cement, building materials, heavy imported commodities, minerals and citrus. The whole network is operated and managed from Haifa.

AIR

El Al, Israel Airlines Ltd, was incorporated on 15 November 1948, as the flag carrier of the new state. Whereas the wisdom of a small country bearing the heavy financial burden of an air fleet was questioned, the geopolitical situation made it necessary for Israel to forge links with friendly nations. Land transport was difficult, if not prohibitive, and sea lanes were slow and subject to disruption. Moreover, foreign air services to the country were uncertain in times of war, as the events of 1956 and 1967 proved when El Al flights were the only ones to be maintained to and from Israel. The economic and social arguments for a national airline were equally pressing; these included the saving in foreign exchange and the advantage it offered in exploiting Israel's tourist potential. A ready passenger market was provided by the large numbers of European and Middle Eastern Jews emigrating to Israel, and El Al became responsible for their mass transportation, including the 'Magic Carpet' operation bringing Jews from the Yemen and the mass shipment of Iraqi Jews.

In spite of the valid reasons underlying its foundation, El Al was expected to operate profitably and not prove to be a financial burden on the state. Eighty per cent of the initial stock was government owned and the other shareholders included the Jewish Agency, the Histadrut and the shipping company Zim. El Al's first European services were to Rome and Paris in August 1949, using a fleet of war surplus UCC-46s and Douglas UCDC-4s. In 1950 the network was extended to include London, Zurich, Vienna, Athens, Istanbul and Nicosia, and a route to South Africa was also inaugurated. Handicapped by old aircraft, El Al maintained a loyal ethnic market, with Jews making up 90 per cent of its passengers. In 1951 the company acquired its first pressurised aircraft (three Lockheed Constellations) and the twice-weekly flights to North America, via London, began operation. Aircraft replacement has been the order of the day (Bristol Britannias in 1957 and then Boeing 707s) and El Al has steadily improved its share in the overall transatlantic market.

El Al's fleet of jet aircraft now spans four continents with regular scheduled services to Western Europe, the United States, Cyprus, Iran and South Africa, and with planned extensions to South America, East Asia and the Antipodes. Air freight has also substantially increased and air transport is particularly valuable for certain export branches, such as diamonds, flowers and fruit. The table below illustrates the growth of international passenger and freight traffic between 1950 and 1970.

Ben Gurion (formerly Lod) is the country's principal airport for El Al and all foreign airlines. Situated 18 kilometres from Tel Aviv and 52 kilometres from Jerusalem, its runways are equal to the needs of the latest jet airliners and the airport's navigational aids, maintenance and repair works are geared to international standards. Ben Gurion is also the telegraphic communications centre for the whole of the country. As a result of the Arab boycott and the prohibition of planes overflying their territories to and from Israel, Ben Gurion is a terminal rather than a transit airport. Only a few airlines continue to Asia using a detour over Turkey and Iran, but the occupation of Sinai has provided a direct route to Africa. The reunification of Jerusalem has resulted in Qalandia airport being prepared for international flights.

BEN-GURION AIRPORT	1950	1960	1970
Aircraft landing	2,272	2,926	9,079
Passengers arriving	82,796	111,602	603,300
Passengers departing	33,846	111,818	586,300
Freight unloaded (tons)	1,410	1,486	12,452
Freight loaded (tons)	536	2,030	913,600

Domestic air travel

Arkia (Israel Inland Airlines) is the country's domestic company. Founded in 1950 by El Al and Kanfot (Wings)—an aviation holding owned by the Histadrut—some of its flight personnel and technical assistance are provided by El Al which owns 50 per cent of the company's stock. Arkia's first route connected Lod with Eilat, but traffic has varied considerably over the years depending on the construction work and other activities at the port. Initially, cargo was a major source of revenue and flights to Eilat were loaded with drinking water, fuel, meat, vegetables and other necessities of life. The completion of the improved road linking Eilat with Tel Aviv and the north meant the decline of this trade since refrigerated trucks were able to transport produce more cheaply. The road link also enabled the bus line to provide better services. Within the last decade Eilat's popularity as a winter resort with Israelis and also with Europeans, particularly the British and Scandinavians, has regenerated air traffic. But construction of an international airport at Eilat, as proposed at one stage, would cut deeply into Arkia's tourist business.

In 1956, the company began a service to Haifa and in 1959 the route was extended to Rosh Pina, north of Lake Kinneret. From time to time Beersheba has been a point of call on the route to Eilat and non-scheduled flights operate to scattered outposts in the Negev. The 1967 June War greatly improved the situation and profitability of Arkia. The reunification of Jerusalem and the occupation of West Bank Jordan placed the most important religious shrines, as well as Jerusalem's principal airport, under Israeli control. This major source of new, short-haul traffic was complemented in 1970 by the operation of a long-haul route to Sharm-el-Sheikh at the southern tip of Sinai. Tours were developed to Sinai and other desert areas, including Masada, and also to the Golan Heights.

SHIPPING

The development of Israeli shipping owes a great deal to the British, not least to the many hundreds of men who learned their seamanship by enlisting in the Royal Navy during World War II. The most important heritage from the mandate, however, is Haifa, which until 1965 served as the only deep-water port on Israel's Mediterranean coast. Haifa was naturally the scene of the country's dramatic expansion in shipping, which was achieved largely through the aid of German reparation payments. Israel's four old vessels in 1948, with a total dead-weight of 6,000 tons, have been replaced by a modern fleet, which in 1971 consisted of 119 ships with a deadweight of 3·3 million tons. This fleet is composed of passenger or mixed-passenger cargo vessels, dry cargo vessels and tankers. In 1971 Zim Navigational Company, the largest of Israel's shipping lines, owned seventy-eight vessels with a total capacity of 1·6 million tons. The company was founded in 1945 by the Jewish Agency, the Histadrut and the Israel Maritime League. Other major shipping companies are Maritime Fruit Carriers and El Yam.

A shipping bank aids the growth of maritime assets, and the Israel Nautical College at Acre trains officers and engineers to meet merchant marine requirements. Israel derives considerable foreign revenue as a sea-carrier, but there have been indications that expansion in shipping has been too dramatic for the state of the market. In recent years financial losses have forced companies to dispose of older vessels or cancel orders for new ones.

Several Mediterranean ports, including Marseilles, Genoa, Naples, Brindisi and Piraeus, operate shipping routes to Israel, but at present the only direct sailings from Britain are by cargo-passenger ships.

PORTS

Haifa, Ashdod and Eilat, the major ports, are managed, maintained and developed by the Israel Ports Authority, founded in 1961. Haifa remains the most significant, its harbour being one of the finest in the eastern Mediterranean.

Haifa

The main harbour, about one square kilometre in area, is enclosed by two breakwaters, while an auxiliary harbour to the east, opened at the mouth of the Kishon river in 1955, is limited to vessels with drafts of 24ft. Good anchorage is also provided in Haifa Bay.

When the port was developed between 1929 and 1933 the intention was to make it a gateway to Palestine and also to a large section of south-west Asia, serving Jordan and parts of Iraq and Iran. A pipeline from the oilfields of Kirkuk in Iraq, accompanied by a metalled road, reached Haifa in 1936, and oil refineries started production in 1939. Haifa also became the centre of Palestine's railway system, but plans for the construction of a railway line to Iraq were interrupted by World War II and then abandoned with the disruption of land communications with Arab territories. The pipeline from Kirkuk was also closed down. As a result, Haifa was deprived of much of its potential hinterland, and the overconcentration of commercial and industrial activities in the Tel Aviv area relegated the port to an off-centre position in terms of the country's economic needs. This was one of the main reasons for the development of the new port of Ashdod which replaced the small anchorages at Tel Aviv and Jaffa.

In spite of the loss of Haifa's Arab hinterland the increase in economic activity in Israel fostered the continued expansion of the port and its trade. In 1970 it handled 3·6 million tons or 55 per cent of Israel's cargo. Haifa's up-to-date port installations, which include a 10,000 ton floating dock, the Dagon grain silo, coal-handling equipment and large transit sheds, make it a major centre of capital investment, and the concentration of heavy and light industries in the Haifa Bay area is a firm guarantee of the port's future importance. The local industries include shipbuilding and repairing, chemicals and petrochemicals, cement, steel mills and foundries, car-assembly plants and a wide variety of light industries. The oil refineries are located on the banks of the Kishon river and now process crude oil brought by pipeline from Eilat.

Ashdod

Located 37 miles south of Tel Aviv, Ashdod is Israel's second deep-water port. The town, literally carved out of the sand, was established in 1957 and the port began operations at the end of 1965. In 1970 Ashdod handled 2·6 million tons, or 39 per cent of Israel's total cargo, and is expected to expand its activities rapidly as further wharves and facilities are provided. The port is planned to serve the country from the north of Tel Aviv to the southern Negev, and already a number of industrial firms, impressed by its prospects and encouraged by the proximity to Tel Aviv, have set up branches in the town. The facilities of the port include container and ore and bulk terminals, which are especially important for handling the mineral products of the

Negev. Tanker terminals are located at the roadstead at Ashkelon, ten miles to the south.

Eilat

Israel's third port is located at the head of the Gulf of Aqaba (or Eilat). Its development as a gateway for trade with Asia, East Africa and the Antipodes is a major objective. The existence of an overland 'canal' between Israel's two seas, linking Haifa and Eilat, is seen as an alternative and potentially cheaper route than the Suez Canal, and one certainly less subject to the vagaries of Egyptian administration.

In 1948 Eilat represented nothing more than a name on the map and it was not until 1956 that Israel was able to take full advantage of its strategic site. The Sinai Campaign broke the Egyptian blockade of the Straits of Tiran, leading to the Gulf of Aqaba, and freedom of shipping was guaranteed by the presence of UN troops. The 1967 war made Eilat's position considerably more secure.

The first stage in Eilat's modern development was the construction of a road (235 kilometres long) from Beersheba to the potential port. Today this is the lifeline of the town and the chief link between settled Israel and its southern, pioneer frontier. The port, which includes the old natural harbour and a new one opened in 1965, is equipped for bulk exports of phosphates and potash, but also exports a wide variety of industrial products. In return it imports tropical raw materials such as timber, rubber and cocoa. The main function of the harbour is its oil installations which transfer crude oil by pipeline to Haifa and to the new terminal at Ashkelon. In 1970 Eilat handled 413,000 tons of general cargo and a constant rise is anticipated.

In spite of its importance to the national economy the growth of Eilat has been slower than expected. In 1971 its population was 14,600, but efforts to foster economic activity meet with the restraints of its desert environment and isolation. Subsidies have attracted industry and tourist facilities, and subsidised housing and air conditioning are considered as essentials to hold the population. However, water desalination plants, independent power plants, new schools and medical facilities make

Eilat a classic symbol of Israel's refusal to accept limits. Eilat remains the country's back-door, but the Israelis have enough faith in the town to envisage it as a main avenue of entry.

7

How They Learn

EDUCATION justly ranks high among the priorities in Israel and today a complete, but complex and problematic, system has been built up from kindergarten to university, or institutions of similar status. It is based on a number of important laws enacted during the early years of statehood, and on certain tenets that are a continuation of Jewish education in the past. As such it has been shaped partly in response to contemporary needs and partly in conformity to traditional attitudes deeply rooted in the Jewish people. Beyond its importance to the general economic advancement of the country, education is also seen as an indispensable instrument in bridging the 'cultural gap' in Israel and in integrating native-born and immigrant populations. This is no small task and all the resources the country can spare are lavished on the improvement and extension of education facilities, which now account for the third largest item in the national budget, after defence and housing. The major efforts are naturally concentrated on children, but numerous adult courses exist, not only to cement the nation by a common language and outlook, but also to satisfy the average Israeli's thirst for knowledge in both practical and academic subjects. Recent statistics show that 30 per cent of the country's population attends some type of educational institution.

THE DEVELOPMENT OF JEWISH EDUCATION

In many communities of the Diaspora education was, for centuries, primarily religious in its content, with the law and its interpretation as the principal subject of study. As successive waves of immigrants entered Palestine each brought with it some of its own characteristic ideas of what the purpose of education should be and of the types of institutions which should be set up. The introduction of Hebrew as the language of instruction in primary and secondary schools was a fundamental step in the evolution of a more standardised education pattern. As early as 1888 the local school at Rishon le-Zion adopted Hebrew as the teaching medium and in 1892 its use was favoured by Jewish teachers throughout Palestine who supported the language enthusiasts led by Ben Yehuda. The major battles were waged against the foreign philanthropic bodies, the Alliance Israelite, the Anglo-Jewish Association, and particularly the Hilfsverein der Deutschen Juden, who were collectively responsible for the principal secondary schools in the main cities. For both practical and prestige reasons these institutions insisted that school instruction should be given in their respective languages—French, English and German.

The establishment of Palestine's first Hebrew secondary schools, the Herzlia Gymnasium in Tel Aviv and the Rehavia Gymnasium in Jerusalem, played an important part in the Hebrew renaissance, but the language issue assumed grave dimensions in 1913 when the Hilfsverein planned the first polytechnic institution at Haifa. In view of the undeveloped state of the Hebrew language, the Hilfsverein resolved that German was to be the medium of instruction for both technical and general subjects. Jewish reaction to what was then a sensible academic resolution was unprecedented. There were revolts and strikes; thousands of pupils and teachers left schools, and the polytechnic itself was boycotted, remaining for some time as an empty shell.

Jewish education was greatly advanced in 1918 when the Zionist Organisation established a national school system in which Hebrew became the primary language of instruction. Subsequently, the responsibility for schooling passed to the Jewish Agency and in 1932 to Vaad Leumi, although the latter's influence and control was largely nominal since there was a wide latitude about the type of school that should be established and the subjects that were taught. The Education Ordinance of 1933 provided, in very general terms, the broad framework for setting up schools, the registration of teachers, the function of local authorities and government supervision. Primary schools were financed by rates levied on the local Jewish settlements and secondary and vocational schools by foreign Jewish organisations, but with a statutory recognition of Hebrew and the national spirit.

The multi-trend system

The large measure of autonomy characteristic of the mandatory period, together with the endemic Jewish talent for sectional and party division, resulted in education developing under a number of distinct and competing 'trends', each corresponding to the main shades of political and religious opinion. The largest division was the General Trend, which was strongly right-wing in affiliation although it boasted the provision of a secular education without political or religious bias. The Labour Trend combined the several political outlooks represented in the Histadrut and was primarily directed to inculcating knowledge of the socialist movement and its principles. In theory the *Kibbutz* Movement formed part of the Labour Trend, but it also evolved a separate and distinctive educational philosophy. Religion and orthodoxy were represented in the Mizrachi and Agudat Israel trends. The former emphasised traditional religious teaching and observance and a large part of the curriculum was devoted to the Talmud and conventional Jewish learning. Agudat Israel was more extreme, stressing, almost to the exclusion of other knowledge, traditional religious tenets and ritual. For good measure a fifth division was recognised—the No-Trend which was eclectic.

The multi-trend system was the cause of much dispute and confusion. Each trend had its own administrative staff and inspectors and, apart from the waste such multiplication involved, the fact that party interests could be made to override pedagogical ones was not beneficial to education progress. Towards the end of the mandatory period the British government set up a committee to survey Jewish education and to report on its possible unification. It proposed the abolition of the trend system, but the mandate was terminated before this and other recommendations could be effectively implemented.

State education

Soon after independence the government's basic policy, as approved by the Knesset in the act of 1949, called for free compulsory education for all children (Jews and Arabs) from the ages of five to fourteen and for all boys aged fourteen to eighteen who, for various reasons, had failed to finish elementary school. This was followed in 1952 by the State Education Act which attempted to abolish the trends by providing a unified public school system under government control. The supervision and organisation of the state elementary schools was vested in the Ministry of Education, which also laid down a standard curriculum but provided for local variations by allowing the inclusion of supplementary subjects up to one-quarter of the whole timetable. No attempt was made to prevent privately owned schools, or those maintained by municipalities and other public bodies, from functioning autonomously. These remained free to work outside the network of state schools, but their curriculum, teaching standards and buildings were approved by the ministry.

Today the country is divided into four school districts and the ministry is responsible for the appointment of teachers, the payment of salaries and for the content of subjects and examinations. Maintenance of school buildings and equipment is the responsibility of the local municipalities which are also in charge, with government support, of all ancillary services such as health, child care and youth organisations. Outside the field of primary education it is only recently that attempts have been made to secure uniformity in more advanced grades.

The two education acts considerably improved and simplified Israel's public education, but many vestiges of the old trend system remain. Provision is made for religious education by the existence of two parallel elementary sections—state and state religious schools—and parents are given free choice in the enrolment of their children. Further diversions from the general pattern include the largely distinct *kibbutz* system and that of Agudat Israel, which continues to teach on strictly orthodox lines. The Agudat schools belong to the category of 'recognised non-official schools' and 85 per cent of their budget is provided by the ministry. They contain roughly 5·5 per cent of the primary school population. Throughout the country there are also a large number of foreign and local private schools belonging to various missionary societies and ecclesiastical organisations.

The further restructuring of the school system is covered by a series of reforms approved by the Knesset in 1969. They call for the gradual extension of free compulsory education and the creation of a six-year primary period followed by a six-year secondary or post-primary period. The first stage in this development, extending compulsory education to the age of fifteen, was implemented between 1969 and 1972, and the second stage will be completed by 1975. Another development is the subdivision of secondary education into intermediate and senior sections and, as far as possible, it is planned that secondary education should be comprehensive. The reforms also include the abolition of the *seker*, the nationwide examination which served as a guide and entry qualification to higher institutions. Under the new system all pupils on completing primary schooling will automatically pass into the junior secondary school without examinations. Further progress, however, will depend on selection committees and professional counselling.

PRIMARY SCHOOLING

Israel's major and continuing problem in primary education is the enormous increase in the school population. This is the result of immigration, the high birth-rate among many immigrant families, and the low infant mortality consequent on improved health services. Children under fifteen years of age make up the largest age group of the population and attendances at primary schools now total in excess of 500,000. Of these, 66 per cent attend the general state schools, 28 per cent religious state schools and the remaining six per cent the schools of Agudat Israel and those run by independent bodies.

Mass immigration has created a chronic shortage of teachers and a grave lack of accommodation and equipment. In the early days of the state all manner of substitute premises were adapted for teaching purposes and it was common for classes to be held in two shifts under canvas, in tin huts, or even in the open. To combat the teacher shortage many graduates from secondary schools were brought into the profession after a teaching and guidance course of only six months. The Israel Defence Forces provided hundreds of young women as language, arts and handicraft teachers for kindergarten and primary schools. The problem of supply and demand continues and, although Israel has largely eliminated unsuitable school buildings, the provision of adequate staff remains a serious challenge. The teaching profession is regarded as hard work for poor pay, but consistent efforts to improve its social and professional image has stimulated entry into teachers' training colleges and institutes of education at the universities. Special preparatory classes and well-paid scholarships are offered as incentives, and the number of unqualified teachers has been substantially reduced. A common characteristic of the profession is its growing feminisation—70 per cent of teachers in primary schools and 43 per cent in secondary being women.

Educational and cultural differences

The divergent national and cultural backgrounds of schoolchildren have provided equally serious sociological problems. Both the initial one year at kindergarten and the subsequent periods of primary schooling are seen as vital forces in levelling out cultural standards, and basic language, science, history and arts are taught from an early age. It is through the children that the ideals and values of the state, which is a definite philosophy of the educational system, have reached immigrant parents, influencing changes in their outlook and habits. This has been amply demonstrated in the case of the Hebrew language where children are often the best teachers of adults. The educational curriculum, however, also has a strongly practical bent; manual work in school gardens and workshops is correlated with present-day needs and with Israel's basic agricultural and manufacturing problems.

The major significant educational differences occur between

children of oriental and western origin, and equality is difficult
to maintain. The school system was devised largely along European lines and until recently failed to cater for oriental needs.
Sixty per cent of the population falls into the category known as
'disadvantaged'—the poor and educationally backward—and
it is on this section that the government is now concentrating its
efforts and resources. One reason for raising the school-leaving
age and for restructuring the educational programme is the rea-
lisation that the root of under-achievement lies in the long
period spent in elementary school where differences in background and performance become entrenched and difficult to
eradicate in the subsequent four years at secondary school.

In practice 60 per cent of oriental pupils were drop-outs in
the early stages of their secondary education. The Home Intervention Programme for Pre-school Youngsters (HIPPY) is
designed to tutor young children in 'disadvantaged' immigrant
families. Educational material is supplied to the mother who
spends fifteen minutes a day with the child as a preparation for
more formal schooling. The scheme has proved successful as an
'early warning' system, revealing both serious learning handi-
caps and potential academic capabilities. Other special projects for oriental children include the combining of general
education with vocational training, particularly in the development towns, and the provision of longer school days and an extended school year. The extra time is utilised for additional
teaching, guided reading, and instruction in the arts and social
activities. The adaptation of basic text-books, audio-visual
teaching and the provision of special in-service training for
teachers of backward children are all part of the concerted
effort to even out the educational and cultural gap.

SECONDARY EDUCATION

Until recently, secondary education was neither compulsory
nor free, but the school reforms pursued since 1969 have considerably altered this picture. Financial assistance for secondary education is given through government and local authority
grants which are made on a sliding scale according to the

parents' means and obligations. The amount of state aid increases annually; about 50 per cent of pupils now receive free education and the remainder are subsidised. This has greatly modified the character of secondary education where formerly the majority of pupils came from higher income, and generally 'western,' families. Children in development towns are particularly favoured, and scholarships and generous financial terms are offered to poor oriental and new immigrant families. Universal free education at secondary level, however, remains an urgent goal.

The academic schools adhere to the curricula recommended by the Ministry of Education and submit to its supervision. The courses lead towards the *bagrut* (matriculation) examination which is the necessary means for entry into institutions of higher education, although the obligation of national service precludes students from moving on much before the age of twenty-one. The introduction of 'streaming' or 'grouping' has been one attempt to improve the structure of academic secondary schooling. It aims at the establishment of two different matriculation examinations and diplomas, one certifying that the holder is a graduate of a secondary school and therefore eligible to attend an institution of higher education, and the other, covering students not wishing to stand for the *bagrut*, is a certificate of completion of the secondary course. This dual system has been designed to discourage drop-outs in the higher grades of secondary education. Another revolutionary development dealing with drop-outs is the centre of pre-academic studies organised by the Hebrew University. This admits more than 1,000 potential degree students a year from culturally deprived backgrounds. Many are unable to express themselves verbally or in writing and they undergo a rigorous eleven-month course of teaching conducted in small tutorial groups. In 1973 a large proportion of the students, 360 of whom were female, moved on to higher technical and academic studies.

Vocational and agricultural schools, administered by the Ministries of Labour and Agriculture respectively, make up 50 per cent of all secondary institutions. Vocational teaching consists of something like twenty hours' practical teaching each week, together with twenty-four hours of instruction in industrial and general subjects. Vocational schools are also attended by day-release students, the latter governed by the Apprentice Act which requires three to four years' apprenticeship in most trades and attendance at school one day a week. Since 1955, a programme for pre-vocational training of pupils in the last two years of state primary schools has operated. Instruction is given in trades; handicrafts and agriculture, and this enables pupils moving on to vocational schools to commence their studies at second-year level. The agricultural schools play an important part in practical education and a special agricultural matriculation has been instituted for enrolment in the Faculty of Agriculture at the Hebrew University.

Orthodox schools

The ultra orthodox groups, which opted out of the state system, have maintained a high degree of separateness in education, with teaching devoted largely to the study of Jewish traditional writings. The major part of their budgets are controlled by the state, however, and a recent innovation is the combination of modern subjects with religious studies, and pupils are prepared for the matriculation examination. Harmonising the scientific and technological spirit of the twentieth century with rules and laws fashioned several thousand years ago is a formidable task. It is interesting that applications to the religious schools exceeds the places they can offer; in 1972 enrolment numbered 18,000. Many schools receive endowments from Europe and the United States which enable them to offer free board and lodging to pupils. The majority of orthodox schools and colleges are in Jerusalem, from which students emerge with qualifications for further training as rabbis or religious teachers.

ARAB EDUCATION

Education is chief among the agencies which are transforming the life of the Arabs in Israel and in no sphere of activity has progress been more rapid. Prior to 1948 only 30 per cent of Arab children attended primary school and the drop-out rate was high, particularly among girls who rarely went beyond the first two or three grades. Today the picture is quite different. Arab education is governed by the same laws and provisions as those for Jewish schools and the percentage of Arab children successfully completing primary education is the highest in the Middle East. Practically every Arab boy attends school and the rapid increase in the percentage of girls in primary and post-primary institutions is a reflection of the higher living standards of the Arab population and its changing attitudes towards education. The Ministry of Education has made consistent efforts to bring the Arab girl into the orbit of state schooling and to combat the tendency for her early drop-out. Arab prejudice to co-education still exists, but mixed classes at the kindergarten stage are gradually easing the way to co-education at higher levels. The majority of Arab schools, however, have separate sections for boys and girls from grade four onwards.

The school curriculum is basically the same as that of Jewish schools except that Arabic is the language of instruction and Moslem and Christian teachings replace that of Judaism. It was the pressure of Arab opinion, however, that induced the government to introduce Hebrew as a language of study in Arab primary schools. This was seen as vital to job prospects and to achieving, in practice, the position of equality with Jews which the law prescribes. The many private Arab schools also adopt the state curriculum and are supervised and financially supported by the Ministry of Education, as are the schools of the Negev maintained for the semi-nomadic Bedouin.

One of the main difficulties in meeting the present desire of the Arab community for improved education is the acute shortage of trained teachers. Many enticements are offered to attract personnel to the profession and generous grants and loans are offered to students of the new Arab teachers' training college in Haifa. For secondary education, some Arabs attend Christian parochial schools or Jewish academic and vocational schools. In the latter, parallel classes for Arabs and Jews are organised although the number of vocational schools for the Arab community has greatly increased in recent years.

KIBBUTZ EDUCATION

A distinctive system of schooling, closely interwoven with its own specific social structure and philosophy, has developed in the *kibbutz* and, to a lesser extent, in the *moshav*. Varying in precise detail between the settlements, the system rests on basic tenets and assumptions which include the emphasis on collective ideals and the necessity of freeing women from traditional home and family ties for equal work and status with men. From the crêche to the secondary school, *kibbutz* education trains children with a character and knowledge that will equip them to live contentedly and creatively in a communal society. A lively interest in social and cultural life is also encouraged to prevent the feeling of boredom and isolation which are often the main reasons for leaving the land.

The formal educational pattern is based on five separate, but progressive, frameworks. After the birth of a child and the subsequent period of rest, the mother returns to her ordinary duties and functions in work and society, and the infant is cared for by trained and experienced nurses. From the infants' house the children are moved to the toddlers' section where they remain until their fourth year. They are placed in play groups of around six children, each with a permanent nurse, and meet their parents during the afternoons. Between the ages of four and seven the children live in kindergartens and then move to the primary division (seven to twelve years) where groups of around twenty live in special quarters with a matron and a teacher-leader. In the final, secondary division, academic and social activities become particularly important. Each group has its special instructor, acting as a type of youth movement leader, and teaching stresses subjects connected with agriculture. Children in the final grade take full part in the working and social life of the *kibbutz* and are formally admitted into the community at the age of eighteen.

The general school curriculum resembles that of the state system, but instruction is shaped by the ideological orientations of the *kibbutz* movement and the larger organisations of which it is a part. Non-selection is its chief characteristic and every child is entitled to all the educational facilities the community provides. Within its own framework no grades are given or examinations held, the philosophy being that in the ideal set-up there is no need for external recognition of talent since children remain in the *kibbutz* in natural succession to their parents and elders. Today, however, this is not universally the case and the system is changing rapidly, and often radically. *Kibbutzim* now find it expedient to teach towards the external state matriculation, and higher education, once rare for *kibbutz* children, is also firmly on the agenda. Educationalists, searching for new ways of teaching the younger generation, have debated at length the merits and failings of the *kibbutz* method. Whether the system is successful even to its own aims is arguable and it is likely that other radical innovations will be introduced in the near future.

ADULT EDUCATION

The Jewish reverence for learning, partly as an end in itself, partly as a means to economic and social advancement, is amply demonstrated in Israel's highly developed programme of adult education. In 1970 over 30,000 adults attended classes that are held in almost every town and village; of this total, 7,000 were studying at evening secondary schools for the official matriculation examination. Initially, adult education was specifically connected with the problems of new immigrants and was limited to the teaching of new skills, the Hebrew language, and basic information about the state and its functioning. Today, adult education has been extended to provide instruction in all branches of science and the humanities, as well as in applied arts, crafts and hobbies. Classes are organised by the Ministry of Education and the universities, and by such variegated bodies as the Histadrut, the Jewish Agency and the Israel Defence Forces.

A unique contribution in the field of adult education is the Israeli-developed *Ulpan*—an institute designed specifically for the cultural integration of immigrants and for the teaching of

Hebrew by rapid modern methods. Nearly 100 *Ulpanim* of various types exist throughout the country, all offering intensive language courses. The prevalent type is the residential, or boarding, *Ulpan* which is particularly popular with professional people. The course lasts five months with classes in Hebrew for five hours a day. The work *Ulpan* is organised in various *kibbutzim* and is planned for younger people. In a course lasting six months, students work four hours a day and study the rest of the time. The day *Ulpan* is attended by students once a week and the popular *Ulpan* organises morning or evening classes, usually under the supervision of local authorities.

In spite of the availability of these intensive language methods a large segment of the immigrant population finds modern Hebrew frustratingly difficult. 'Learning a Month' is a scheme where a language instructor visits a home in which a number of adults meet for study and conversation. As a further aid to the immigrant, daily and weekly newspapers are published in simplified and 'vowelled' Hebrew, and lessons and news bulletins in basic Hebrew are broadcast over the radio.

Within the context of adult education the activities of the army deserve special attention. The fact that many immigrants are enlisted shortly after arriving in Israel poses major educational and cultural problems. The army's Department of Education provides primary, secondary, vocational and adult education courses as well as intensive instruction in Hebrew. It also co-operates in reinforcing the teaching body by deferring the mandatory service for girls until they graduate from teachers' training college. At the discretion of the Ministry of Education they may be drafted as uniformed counsellors or literacy teachers.

HIGHER EDUCATION

Israel's continued economic and social progress depends to a large extent on its ability to train scholars, professional people, scientists and technicians of high calibre. It is significant, therefore, that the country's main institutions of higher education—the Israel Institute of Technology (the Technion) at

Haifa, and the Hebrew University of Jerusalem—date back to 1912 and 1918 respectively, when the modern development of the Jewish community was still in its embryonic form. Today Israel relies on additional higher institutions—the rapidly expanding University of Tel Aviv, the Bar-Ilan University of Ramat Gan, which is a religious foundation, the University of Haifa and the University of the Negev at Beersheba.

With the exception of the Negev university, whose courses are under the academic supervision of other institutions, the universities and colleges are autonomous foundations, free to conduct their own academic and administrative affairs. In 1972 the combined student enrolment was 45,000 and university education is marked by a high degree of enthusiasm among both students and staff. Seventy per cent of their annual budgets are met by the government and the Jewish Agency, but Israeli universities are under pressure to expand; they need more money, teachers, buildings, scholarships and land for sports and cultural facilities. A persistent phenomenon is the adverse effect of the 'brain drain', mainly to America.

The Hebrew University plays a cardinal role in Israel's intellectual and academic leadership and serves as the formal apex of the education system. It is both the pride and wonder of the country and the finest institution of its kind in the Middle East. The university was founded on Mount Scopus in 1918 and was opened by Lord Balfour in 1925. Initially, it was mainly a research institution, but growing demands led to the development of regular university teaching departments and faculties. In 1948 Mount Scopus was cut off from the rest of Israel and the campus and the adjoining Hadassah Hospital existed as a small enclave in Jordanian territory. Under the terms of truce Israel was to retain ownership and have access to both institutions, but Jordan interpreted this as allowing a ritual inspection a few times a month by Israeli officials and a UN escort. The buildings remained unoccupied until the recapture of Mount Scopus in 1967 and the university was housed in varied premises—convents, schools and offices—in and around Jerusalem. The pressing need for better accommodation led to the decision to build a new campus on a 125-acre site at Givat Ram in the western suburbs of Jerusalem. This is now a university city, maintained by funds raised by Jews abroad, government grants and tuition fees. Its financial deficit, however, is said to be the largest of any university in the world, but it exists and functions because it must, as the intellectual and professional voice of the country. In 1968, work began on the redevelopment of the Mount Scopus site. Provision has been made for hostels and residences, as shortage of accommodation and high rents have made the lot of the student in Jerusalem a difficult one.

In 1972 the Hebrew University had over 16,000 students (1,000 in 1948) and its teaching philosophy is the maintenance of a balance between scholarship and practical needs. Together with the humanities, education, Jewish studies, and Asian and African studies, instruction and research are carried out in the natural and physical sciences, medicine, law, social sciences and agriculture. A special medical course has been organised by the Hadassah Medical School for students from developing countries. It is supported by the World Health Organisation.

Science, both pure and applied, has long been highly esteemed among the Jews, who have contributed significantly to its progress in many countries of the Diaspora. In Israel, the provision for its study is correspondingly liberal and the foundations of this were laid during the mandatory period with the development of the Haifa (now Israel) Institute of Technology. Originally conceived as a building-trade school with faculties of architecture and building technique, the Technion enlarged its vision in the 1920s to meet the demands that mass immigration made on the technological resources of the country. In 1953 the Technion was transferred from its old congested quarters in Hadar Hacarmel to a 300-acre campus on Mount Carmel itself, which also contains a junior technical college and a technical high school. In 1972 its student enrolment was 5,400 full-time undergraduates and 2,600 working for higher degrees or on research projects financed by the government and other bodies. Around 600 graduates are turned out each year and the Technion has been responsible for producing most of Israel's scientists and engineers. Mount Carmel also houses the first buildings of Haifa University, founded in 1963. It has faculties of humanities and social sciences, schools of education and social work and institutes of biology and maritime studies. In

1972 there were over 5,000 students (380 Arabs and Druzes) and a teaching staff of 460.

The University of Tel Aviv occupies a large campus in the northern suburb of Ramat Aviv and in 1972 had a student population of 12,000 and an academic staff of 1,800. It was founded in 1956 as a municipal institution and formerly housed a number of departments of the Hebrew University. A successful bid for autonomy was made in the 1960s, since when the university has expanded rapidly.

Another fast-growing infant (although not an autonomous institution), is the University of the Negev at Beersheba. Courses in the faculties of humanities, social sciences and engineering come under the academic supervision of the Hebrew University, the Technion and the Weizmann Institute. In 1971 there were 1,700 undergraduates, 150 postgraduates and a teaching staff of 350. Many of the latter are employed on a temporary basis and air-service links between Haifa, Jerusalem, Tel Aviv and Beersheba make possible the mutual exchange of staff. The first degrees were awarded in 1969.

Religious orthodoxy has its own well-equipped institution of higher learning in the Bar-Ilan University at Ramat Gan. It was founded by the Mizrachi party in 1955 and named after the religious Zionist leader, Rabbi Meir Bar-Ilan. This is not a theological institution but a fully-fledged university in its own right with faculties of Jewish studies, social sciences, mathematics, and schools of education and social work. Teachers and students are observant Jews and Jewish studies are a compulsory part of the curriculum. Of the 6,000 students a large section come from abroad, and branches of the university operate at Ashkelon, Safad and Tzemach.

Research institutes

Applied research and services to industry are conducted from the majority of Israeli universities and colleges. The Technion, for example, offers consulting and testing facilities to industry, quality control and technological surveys. The most notable research centre, however, is the Weizmann Institute of Science at Rehovot, which developed from the modest Daniel

Sieff Research Institute, founded in 1934. Dedicated in 1949 to Israel's first president, himself a firm advocate of the importance of science to the nation, the institute achieved a rapid programme of expansion, largely as the result of foreign beneficiaries. Research is carried out in nineteen departments, which are grouped into the faculties of biology, biophysics and biochemistry, chemistry, mathematics and physics. The institute's community numbers some 1,850 which include over 400 scientists, 480 students attached to the Feinberg Graduate School and a number of foreign exchange or guest fellows. The Yeda Research and Development Company deals with the commercial promotion of industrially promising research projects developed at the institute.

The Volcani Institute of Agricultural Research is also located at Rehovot. It was set up in 1921 by the Jewish Agency and was taken over by the Ministry of Agriculture in 1951. The institute's main departments are concerned with soil science, irrigation, plant experimentation and protection, applied botany and livestock research. Its main contributions to research have included the discovery of plants adaptable to desert conditions, and methods of anchoring sand dunes. The institute administers over 600 research projects and an experimental farm is located between Rehovot and Tel Aviv.

Israel is fully aware that the natural deficiencies of the country have to be compensated by the results of advanced scientific research. It is coordinated by the National Council for Scientific Research and Technological Development, which finances projects and awards fellowships. Experiments peculiarly pertinent to the country include water desalination, harnessing solar energy, electricity by wind-power, electrical properties in soils, desert agriculture, artificial cloud-seeding, pilot plant studies and environmental physiology.

8

How They Amuse Themselves

WITH a long working week of six or, at best, five-and-a-half days, heavy taxation and low real incomes by American and Western European standards, the average Israeli has neither time nor money to squander on expensive entertainments. This is not to suggest that a wide variety of amusements and pastimes do not exist, or that the Israelis are incapable of enjoying themselves. On the whole, they prefer to spend their leisure time in cultural activities or in outdoor and sporting events. Night clubs and discotheques, which obviously appeal to the younger generation, are found in such unlikely sounding places as Nazareth, Eilat and Beersheba, but night-life is not highly developed. Even in Tel Aviv—Jaffa, the entertainment capital, night clubs have been described as closer in spirit to YMCA's than to the ribald dens of iniquity one associates with Beirut or Cairo. Israel's nearest equivalents are the oriental night spots of East Jerusalem, patronised by tourists.

Such 'worldly' amusements have been criticised by the country's religious backing, as indeed were discotheques and espresso coffee shops in the 1960s, but it is possibly the Israelis' disinterest in alcohol that accounts for the low popularity of lascivious entertainment. Alcoholic drinks are obtainable in hotels, restaurants and cafés but, with the exception of those catering exclusively for foreign colonies, there are few pubs or bars resembling those in Britain and the United States. Few Israelis drink anything stronger than beer, preferring coffee, tea, fruit juice or the ubiquitous Coca-Cola. Much of the comedy and drama of daily life takes place out of doors and the pavement café provides a convenient rendezvous and forum for discussion and debate, as well as a place for sitting and observing the world go by. Café life is developed on all levels and the morning congregation of 'bourgeoisie' women in middle-class districts of Tel Aviv, Haifa and Jerusalem is a custom not unlike that of Vienna, Munich, Rome and other European cities.

Any lack of interest in alcohol is more than compensated for by the Israelis' love of betting. This is a major form of escape and a variety of sporting pools and a national lottery operate. Lottery tickets, which may win as much as £20,000 ($46,000), are sold from pavement kiosks or by itinerant street sellers.

FESTIVALS AND HOLIDAYS

For the majority of the population the weekly period of rest and relaxation is the Shabbat (Sabbath) which starts, in effect, after 2 pm on Friday afternoon and lasts until Saturday evening. There is little public transport during this period, except in Arab areas and in Haifa; places of entertainment, apart from a number of restaurants, also close. The way in which Shabbat is observed depends on religious convictions. There is little sign of enjoyment in the Mea Shearim district of Jerusalem where even private cars are banned, but for the less orthodox the Shabbat, if a day of rest, is not necessarily kept 'holy'. Only a minority of the population is strictly orthodox, but a number of Jewish religious festivals are annually celebrated as national holidays—though not everywhere according to the ancient religious rituals.

The two days of Rosh Hospanah in late September or early October celebrate the Jewish New Year. This is followed ten days later by Yom Kippur, the Solemn Feast of Atonement, which in reality is marked by fasting and prayer, and is the most sacred day in the Jewish year. Succoth, the Feast of the Tabernacles, is also a harvest festival and commences a few days after Yom Kippur. It commemorates the time when the Children of Israel wandered in the wilderness and many orthodox Jews eat their meals in leafy huts, adorned with vegetables and fruits, erected in gardens or on balconies. The eighth day of Succoth ends with Simkhat Torah, 'rejoicing in the Law', when the final section of the Torah, followed immediately by the beginning, is read in synagogues. Chanacuh (November or December) is the Hebrew Festival of Lights and celebrates the triumph of the Maccabean revolt. Its symbol is the seven-branch candelabrum (*menorah*) and one candle is lit each night throughout the ceremonial period. The festival of Purim falls in February or March and commemorates Esther's preservation of the Babylonian Jews. Apart from religious services, it is a *mardi gras* type of holiday replete with fancy-dress parades, masked balls and exchanges of gifts. Its climax is the great carnival festival in Tel Aviv. The Passover is celebrated at about the same time as the Western Christian Good Friday. It commences with the Seder meal, during which the Hagadah is read, retelling the story of the Exodus. The first and last days are Holy Days while the intervening period is a semi-holiday.

The most important non-religious event is Independence Day (14 May 1948) which is marked by parades, speeches, picnics and sporting occasions. Folk-dancing is a main feature of all religious and secular festivals and Israel's national dance, the Hora, appears to be derived from Russian and East European countries.

In addition to Jewish Holy Days and holidays all the major Christian feasts are celebrated twice over—once on the dates used by the Western (Roman Catholic and Protestant) Churches, and again on the Eastern (Orthodox) Churches' dates. To round off this tally of religious festivals there are also a large number of Moslem and Druze celebrations. The Moslem Sabbath is Friday, but Moslem businesses do not close down as completely as Jewish concerns on Saturdays and Christian establishments on Sundays.

OUTDOOR AND SPORTING ACTIVITIES

The importance of outdoor activities to the Israelis is revealed in their concern for the natural and historical heritage of the country. There are some fifty sites (many already open to the public) designated by the National Parks Authority, which was established in 1963 to replace the functions carried out from 1956 by the Department of Landscaping and the Preservation of Historic Sites. Most of the national parks have been linked with the country's major historical remains and since 1968 the annual number of visitors has exceeded two million. The rapid development of the country has inevitably affected plant and animal ecology and the Nature Reserves Authority was established in 1963 to provide natural areas for both public access and scientific observation.

Many societies combine professional interests with cultural and educational activities; two that are associated with the natural and cultural landscape are the Society for the Protection of Nature and the Israel Exploration Society. Youth movements are also active in the extra-curriculum education and recreation of young people, mainly between the ages of ten and sixteen. The Ministry of Education and Culture and the Youth and Pioneering Department of the World Zionist Organisation help the movements to train leaders and organise libraries, camps and other facilities for their members. The Israel Scout Federation of 22,000 members is just one of the wide variety of youth and pioneering movements, and Jewish and Arab scouts have participated in international jamborees.

Walking is a major recreation and ramblers' tracks are found in almost every corner of Israel. Vantage points have their carefully tended picnic areas, with tables and benches, litter bins, and sections where fires may be lit. The National Committee for the Friends of Nature in Haifa organises a number of long-distance walks and other annual events, including the spring three-day Jerusalem walk, modelled on Holland's *Vier Daagse*. In 1971, 20,000 soldiers and civilians took part in the walk; other mass events are the 2·5-mile Lake Kinneret swim and the 6-mile cross-country race round Mount Tabor.

All sports in Israel are amateur. Football can be regarded as the national game, although basketball, swimming, athletics, tennis and volleyball have large followings. Swimming and associated water sports (skin and scuba diving and water-skiing) are popular on the coasts and lakes. Underwater exploration is richly rewarded along the coast of eastern Sinai, from Eilat to Ophira, where there is a great variety of tropical fish, corals and archaeological remains.

CULTURAL PURSUITS

Israelis of all ages are profoundly conscious of their historical heritage; archaeology, which amounts to a craze among both professionals and amateurs, combines outdoor adventure with bookish toil. Thousands follow the activities of archaeologists through the extensive press coverage given to new discoveries, by attending lectures and conventions, or by participation in archaeological excavations. There is never a shortage of volunteers to help on an excavation and the country has many outstanding professional archaeologists. Although archaeology is a prominent university discipline, it can also be regarded as Israel's national pastime.

The passion for academic activities is again revealed in an incessant hunger for reading matter. A prominent feature of almost every shopping street is the multiplicity of bookstores and the wide range of stock in terms of subjects and languages. The 100 or so publishing houses produce, on average, 2,000 titles a year. Israel thus has the highest per capita book production in the world, with the exception of Switzerland. Booksellers also find a big demand for books in foreign languages and book imports are proportionately the second highest in the world. The great demand for literature is reflected in the country's 2,000 libraries which collectively contain 13 million books. The largest is the Jewish National and University Library with over 1·5 million volumes. Basic libraries provided by the Ministry of Education and Culture form an essential focal point in new immigrant settlements and in all collective villages.

The Bible, the very core of Jewish existence, remains the most widely read book, its study forming a high percentage of the school curriculum. Jerusalem is one of the foremost world centres of Bible study and research; actively engaged are the Hebrew University, the Rabbi Kook Institute, the Pontifical Biblical Institute and other Christian foundations. Added to these are the Bar-Ilan and Tel Aviv universities and the Bible Institute at Rishon-le-Zion. The Israel Society for Biblical

Research holds lectures, study circles and assemblies throughout the country. The Bible Contests are followed with intense interest by almost the entire population and attract challengers from all over the world.

THE PRESS

Israel's press is as diversified as the population, covering every shade of opinion in a variety of languages. It is free of all political censorship, although control is exercised over matters of security. There are thirteen dailies in Hebrew, two in Arabic and eight in other languages. The two foremost morning papers sell 40–50,000 copies, most of the others ranging from 5,000 to 25,000. The evening papers have larger circulations of 130–160,000. Tel Aviv is the home of all national papers, except the *Jerusalem Post* which was founded in 1932 and tends to reflect a semi-official government position. There are over 400 periodicals, 300 published in Hebrew, fifty in English and the remainder in twelve other languages.

RADIO AND TELEVISION

The Israelis love the radio and in 1971 there were some 600,000 licensed receivers. Music blares out incessantly in cafés, workshops and often, unlawfully, in public transport. Other programmes followed with keen interest are the twenty Hebrew news bulletins sent out daily on the hour.

Radio and television is controlled by the Israel Broadcasting Authority, founded in 1948. The board of governors consists of thirty-one members appointed by the president on the recommendation of the government; there is a management board of seven and a director-general. The authority's four stations broadcast on twenty-five wavelengths for a total of fifty-five hours daily. Light programmes are produced in Hebrew, Arabic, English and French, and there are special programmes for immigrants transmitted in simplified Hebrew and in Yiddish, Ladino, Moghrabi, Russian, Persian and Hungarian.

Dar el Iza'a el Israeliya, the IBA's Arabic station, broadcasts for over fourteen hours a day. It serves the Arabs in Israel, but has many listeners in neighbouring countries and performs an important function in counteracting propaganda.

Public demand for a television service in the late 1950s was initially opposed by the Knesset. Even the Rothschild Trust's offer of a pilot scheme for schools was viewed with suspicion. The government maintained that Israel could not afford television, and that it would be detrimental to the country's productivity and cultural cohesion. An increasing segment of the population was already tuning in to Arab stations on sets that were either bought locally or brought in by immigrants. This, more than anything, forced the hand of the government, which accepted that it was better to be corrupted by indigenous rather than by foreign matter! Programmes for schools were introduced in 1966 and transmission for the general public began in 1968. Israel's first 'official' telecast was the twentieth Independence Day parade in Jerusalem and the second milestone was a concert by the Israel Philharmonic Orchestra conducted by Leonard Bernstein.

Although transmitting is now on a regular basis, with daily programmes in Hebrew and Arabic, television is still in its infant stage and largely experimental. Presentation has been much improved by the training of producers, cameramen, performers and technicians by foreign specialists. A high proportion of the programmes consist of interviews with leading national and international personalities, news coverage and current events. Perhaps it is for this reason that some of Israel's 500,000 (1971) television owners still tune in to Amman and Beirut, which transmit a heavy dose of American, French and Italian films!

CINEMA

The cinema is the chief form of indoor entertainment and the Israelis rank among the most cinema-conscious citizens in the world. Up until 1968 over 65 million tickets were sold annually, which was equivalent to an average attendance per head of population of twenty-five visits a year. With the introduction of television, attendances have dropped by 30 per cent, but this is viewed by the industry as a temporary phase, and cinemas are still among the first buildings to spring up in new settlements and suburban areas. Attendances are highest in Tel Aviv and Haifa, which are the centres of metropolitan regions and therefore attract people from neighbouring towns and villages.

In 1971, Israel had 270 commercial cinemas with a total seating capacity of 185,000. In addition, regular shows are provided in some 600 villages (including *kibbutzim*) and small towns without permanent auditoriums. Most full-length films are imported from the United States, Italy, France and Britain; these are subtitled in Hebrew and generally, if the film warrants it, in English and French also. Tickets, especially for westerns, musicals and detective films—the Israeli favourites— are often purchased in advance from ticket agencies.

Israel's film industry is small, but in recent years it has made considerable progress with a number of films achieving international acclaim and winning awards at film festivals. One index of the industry's increasing maturity is the movement away from purely national subjects (the War of Independence, pioneering and immigration etc) to general subjects of greater appeal to foreign audiences. A large number of short documentaries are also produced. Many of these are sponsored by the government, the Jewish Agency and the Jewish National Fund; television has further stimulated production.

The Israel Film Centre, which functions within the Ministry of Commerce and Industry, is responsible for the promotion and further development of film-making. It authorises tax refunds, customs exemptions and grants for approved feature and short artistic films made in Israel, and it is anxious to encourage foreign film activities within the country. The interest of foreign directors shooting in Israel is related, in part, to the variety of scenic locations within relatively short distances of each other. Other favourable factors include the cultural backgrounds of ancient and modern, oriental and Western, and a climate with almost eight continuous rainless months. Israel has concluded co-production agreements with France, the German Federal Republic, Belgium and Sweden, and further agreements are being negotiated.

THEATRE

Next to the cinema, the theatre is Israel's most popular form of indoor entertainment. A number of professional companies are sustained by public support. All classes of society are theatregoers and attendance per capita is the highest in the world, with over 3 million tickets sold each year for a season that lasts eleven months. The country is small enough to allow the city-based companies to travel almost anywhere in Israel, returning the same night. Even frontier *kibbutzim* enjoy frequent theatrical performances and form the theatre's most faithful audiences.

In 1948 the Israeli theatre consisted of three repertory companies, all located in Tel Aviv. The Habimah (literally 'the stage') was already thirty years old. This Hebrew theatre, originally organised by Nahum Zemach, the actor-pupil of Stanislavsky, was founded in Moscow in 1918. It reached a high standard of artistic achievement under the direction of Vakhtangon and its successful tours, which included Britain and the United States, were major events in the theatrical scene of the 1920s. In 1932 the Habimah settled permanently in Palestine, bringing with it a repertoire of plays which, although concerned with Messianic ideas and Jewish mysticism, constituted an inspiration for modern theatrical development. In 1958, to mark the fortieth anniversary of the theatre and the tenth anniversary of the state, the Habimah was recognised as the Israeli National Theatre, enjoying a substantial government subsidy.

The Othel and the Cameri were the other companies founded prior to independence. The Othel, a co-operative company closely linked with the Histadrut, was founded in 1925 and dedicated to the ideals of the labour movement. For reasons which included rising production costs and competition from other media it broke up in 1969. The Cameri (Chamber) Theatre was established in 1944 as a reaction against the conservatism of the two older companies. Under Josef Milo it trained many young Israel-born and immigrant actors, and began a new era in the Hebrew theatre with its presentation of modern works dealing in a straightforward manner with problems of family, sex and war. On its twenty-fifth anniversary the

Cameri became Tel Aviv's municipal theatre.

Israel's third publicly-sponsored repertory company, the Haifa Municipal Theatre, was founded in the early 1960s. This was the first theatre to be located outside Tel Aviv and the first to be fully subsidised. For a number of years it suffered from a shortage of actors who were magnetised by the theatrical life of Tel Aviv, but today the theatre is adventurous, popular and highly professional. One anomaly in Israel's theatrical life is that Jerusalem, with its capital status and centres of Hebrew study, has been poorly represented in terms of drama. The new Jerusalem Theatre was opened in 1971, but the city's Hebrew productions continue to come from Tel Aviv. English theatre, catering for around 40,000 English-speaking residents and tourists, is well established in the capital and Arab theatrical groups operate in East Jerusalem. In addition to Israel's repertory companies, there are a number of smaller groups, mostly of recent growth and mainly in Tel Aviv, which specialise in revues and avant-garde plays. Commercial companies staging light comedies and American-style musicals are equally appreciated by the Israelis.

Among the problems of the Hebrew theatre is the scarcity of original plays. In an average season only five or six new plays out of some thirty productions are staged. The general theatre is encouraged by the Art for the People organisation, taken over by the government in 1966. It arranges theatrical appearances in new immigrant centres at reduced prices, and works on an annual budget of over £100,000 ($230,000). The government sponsors the drama school at Ramat Gan; drama is also taught in the Hebrew University and at the Department of Theatre Arts in Tel Aviv. In addition there are a number of private centres for training actors, designers and directors.

MUSIC

Of all the arts which flourish in Israel, music has contributed most strikingly to the cultural progress as well as to the international reputation of the country. The Jews are traditionally music-loving, and music instruction and appreciation are part of the curriculum in all schools from kindergarten onwards. Opportunities for specialised training are provided at academies in Jerusalem and Tel Aviv, at the Hebrew University and at numerous conservatoires. The varied ethnic composition of the population is reflected in the types of music which are current. The main problem is to fit Western musical tradition into an environment still largely shaped by the heritage of Jewish sacred melody and by the rhythms of the Hebrew language. The absence of a national, indigenous musical background means that 'classical' music is regarded as the realm of the West, but interest in it is neither an urban nor middle-class monopoly. Orchestral tours and concerts find appreciative audiences in the new towns, *kibbutzim* and frontier villages.

In the classical field the Israel Philharmonic Orchestra is the country's main claim to fame and has provided a powerful incentive to the expansion of musical facilities and education. Founded as the Palestine Symphony Orchestra in 1936 by Bronislav Huberman, it was made up mainly of refugee musicians from leading European orchestras. The Philharmonic was welded into an orchestra of international standing by Toscanini and has performed under such illustrious conductors as Barbirolli, Bernstein, Sargent, Mitropoulos, Ormandy and Paray. The Mann Auditorium in Tel Aviv, with a capacity of 3,000, is the Philharmonic's headquarters. Here it presents the majority of its 200 annual concerts, but a subscription list of 36,000 patrons—a world record percentage of the population—necessitates frequent provincial performances. The orchestra has successfully toured in North America, Western Europe, Australia and New Zealand, including in its international repertoire the works of Israeli composers such as Marc Lavry, Oedeon Partos, Paul Ben-Haim, Joseph Tal and Ben-Zion Orgad.

The Kol Israel Orchestra, based in Jerusalem, is maintained by the Israel Broadcasting Authority. Its programmes of light, popular and classical music cater for a wide public. It concentrates in particular on works of local authorship and compositions usually omitted from the Philharmonic programmes by reason of their limited public appeal or experimental character. Other important orchestras are the

Haifa City Symphony (founded in 1950), the Ramat Gan
Chamber (1954) and those belonging to the Defence Forces
and the *Kibbutz* Movement. Gadna, the pre-military organisation for young people aged fourteen to eighteen, prides itself in a
symphony orchestra which has carried off awards at European
international competitions.

Israel has a great many vocal groups and choirs. Both the
Philharmonic and Kol have their choral sections and in addition there are the Tel Aviv and Haifa Chamber choirs and
numerous student, academy, *kibbutz* and school choral unions.
The Israel National Opera, founded in 1948, now forms a company of around 230, including conductors, soloists, choir, dan-
cers and musicians. The two important ballet companies are
the Bat-Sheva and the Bat-Dor, founded respectively in 1964
and 1968, which have toured extensively abroad. Israeli dance
is perhaps most widely represented by Inbal, a Yemenite group
drawing its material from oriental and biblical themes.

Folk, jazz and pop music have a large following in Israel.
Pop, in particular, is turned out in prodigious quantity, with hit
songs sprouting and wilting in swift succession. Much of this
music is recognisably Israeli, but its main themes are of international appeal—love, springtime, the soldier returning etc.
The folksongs, heard on stage as well as on radio, reflect Israeli
history and experience; the number of amateur folksong groups
increases annually.

In view of the Israelis' love of music it is not surprising that
there are an ever-growing number of music festivals, contests
and seminars. The Israel Music Festival is held annually in
summer and every three years includes the International Harp
Contest. The festival is centred in Jerusalem and at the restored
Roman theatre in Caesarea, though performances take place in
other towns and in *kibbutzim*. Another annual festival is held
during Passover at Ein Gev, a *kibbutz* near Lake Kinneret; its
programme includes classical dance and folk music. A similar
spring festival takes place at Ein Hashofat near Megiddo.
Other festivals are the Zimria, a contest for international
Jewish choirs, and the Dalia festival of folk-dancing.

ART

The Israelis are particularly art conscious and the country is now in an economic position to support art and its artists. The commercial art gallery business in the leading cities and vacation areas is booming, and the number of exhibitions, museums, and private collections is remarkable for a small country. Even modest apartments usually boast one or two original art items.

Tel Aviv, the art capital of the country, abounds in commercial galleries and museums. Jerusalem has been slower to develop its artistic quarters, but a plan to bring the Old City back to its original form and character includes the redevelopment of the Mount Zion area into artists' workshops. A successful artists' quarter, including a night-life centre, has been developed in Old Jaffa. At a cost of £430,000 ($1 million) old houses have been reconstructed and turned into studios for painters, sculptors, weavers and other craftsmen. Other artist colonies include the village of Ein Hod, near Haifa, which is run on a cooperative basis, and the town of Safad with over fifty resident painters and sculptors.

The question of whether there is a national style or a distinctive common denominator in Israeli art is difficult to assess. Painters and sculptors have obviously been influenced by European traditions and the pioneer artists of the early years of this century—Chagall, Epstein, Kisling, Adler, Levine and others—had developed a style that leaned heavily on expressionism. In 1922, however, there were enough artists in Palestine to warrant the establishment of the Association of Painters and Sculptors and by 1927 art galleries were opened in Jerusalem and Tel Aviv. With independence, the expressionist style gave way to the 'New Horizons' movement founded by Janco, Mokady, Mairovich, Stemastsky and Zaritsky. Its doctrine was the advancement of abstract tendencies and other modern ideas, and the movement became associated with similar groups in New York, Rome, London and Paris.

Israel's younger generation of artists—painters such as Bezem, Arikha, Gross, Halevy and Bergner, and sculptors like Shemi, Fima and Turmarkin—are representatives of the many adherents to both the strong abstract and figurative styles. An interesting aspect of the contemporary art scene is the relatively large percentage of successful women artists, a reflection of the equality of artistic opportunity in Israel.

The main source of academic art instruction is the Bezalel Art School in Jerusalem, which is associated with the Bezalel Museum (now part of the Israel Museum) founded in 1906 by Boris Schatz. Techniques and designs in weaving, embroidery, metal-work, wood, glass, ceramics and jewellery are encouraged by the government and the Jewish Agency, largely to provide quality and useful items for the tourist market. Traditional art and craft items can be seen in the many specialist museums in Tel Aviv.

LITERATURE

Hebrew has no continuous literary tradition. As a language it ceased to be widely spoken around AD 200 and for a long period Hebrew appeared only in religious writings in Jewish categorical law, moral and religious sermons and texts, and in the liturgical poetry of the synagogue. There are few examples of Hebrew being used as the mundane language of everyday speech, although there is evidence that it flourished in Moslem Spain in the eleventh and twelfth centuries and in Italy during the Renaissance. The regeneration of Hebrew began in Russia and eastern Europe during the eighteenth century when secular works in prose and poetry appeared after centuries of strictly religious writing. The awakening was concurrent with the birth of Jewish national consciousness, and literature acted as a major stimulant. The literary movement reached its peak with the prose of Sefarim (1835–1917) and the poetry of Bialik (1873–1934). The works of Bialik determined his special place in Hebrew literature as the country's 'national poet' in the full sense of the term. He was called the prophet of chastisement and mercy, for his poetry deals with the tragedy of the Exile and also the Return to Zion.

In the more modern literature of Israel a number of major trends are discernible, each drawing inspiration from varied sources and focussing on different national themes. Agnon and Hazaz provide the links between twentieth-century writing and the 'classical' works of Sefarim and Bialik. Their writings reflect the formidable problems which accompanied the transition from a religious way of life to that of a secular technological Israeli society. Agnon, a Nobel Prize winner in 1966, treats the Jew's problems of adjustment, at varied levels and in varied contexts, in a series of epic stories and Hassidic tales. The work of Hazaz is also founded on dramatic-historical fact, and focal points in his narratives include the Russian Revolution, the implications of World War II on Jewry and the problems emanating from the different cultural setting of Yemenite Jewry. The crisis in Judaism is also the major theme of the poetic works of Greenberg.

The clash of transcendental Judaism with the newly moulded Israeli scene figures less prominently in the literary works of the succeeding generation. Younger writers arriving on the waves of the Second and Third Aliyas rejected the ghetto and Diaspora themes; their novels, poems and plays featured an Israeli life where realism was the keynote. Poets like Alterman, Shlonsky and Goldberg were instrumental in bridging the cultural gap between anachronistic Hebrew and the demotic tongue. They rejected the Ashkenazic dialect for Sephardic and introduced colloquialisms, technological jargon, and coined new terms when required for literary expression. Their major themes, and those of Lamdan, Shalom, Yizhar, Shaham and others, reflect the transition from one country and culture to another, the problems of settling in an alien and barren land, and the feelings of isolation and disappointment in Israel. But they also deal with the processes of reintegration in the spiritual life of the Jews and in this Alterman is the major champion. His verse on political and social themes became one of the country's all-time best-sellers, retailing more than 60,000 copies.

The 'Sabra' writers have gone further in abandoning, even forgetting, the Diaspora foundations of modern Israel. Yehoshua and Oz, in particular, have challenged the idea of indebtedness to the society from which they originated. Many have argued that in such a viewpoint Hebrew literature has reached full circle. What was significant to the writers of the

Diaspora—the breakup of Jewish culture and faith—is now significant to the Sabra writers—the existence of a cultural void from which the integral essence of life is missing. This attitude, however, is not universal and optimism characterises the youngest wave of Israeli poets, the 'flower-children' of Hebrew literature. They have turned to a beautiful, rather baroque type of expression, and the writings represented by Horovitz, Volach and Geldman appear all the more significant against the background of continuous warfare and the feeling of political insecurity in Israel.

Although a large number of dedicated writers exist in Israel, few are able to maintain a livelihood from literature, in spite of the average Israeli's avid interest in books. Writers suffer from dealing with a small public, not all of whom can read and understand Hebrew, and by far the largest book sales come from translations of foreign works. The government annually awards prizes to distinguished authors, but the oldest literary honour is the Bialik Prize, which was inaugurated to promote the Hebrew language and literature, and Jewish studies generally.

9

Hints for Visitors

Israel is what the individual makes it. It is a country of contrasts which either confuse the comprehension or, for those more open to acceptance, provide a rich scenic and varied cultural tabloid to be enjoyed for its own intrinsic value.

The best time of year for visiting Israel depends very much on personal choice. The Israeli summer is long, virtually rainless and the heat can be sweltering. At the height of summer the most pleasant vacation areas are the many Mediterranean resorts and the hill towns of Jerusalem and Safad where the atmosphere is drier and cooler. In summer, light, cool clothes, a head covering and sunglasses are a necessity; for the cooler evenings in the hill country a jacket or sweater is recommended. The winter season, from November to March, is characterised by cooler temperatures and short spells of rain interspersed with long periods of sunshine. During winter, however, the Lake Kinneret area, Sodom on the Dead Sea, and Eilat all have ideal warm sunny weather, but for most parts of Israel rainwear and normal-weight clothing are needed.

Informal dress is the rule rather than the exception. Some of the better hotels and restaurants tend to prefer their guests to wear lounge suits and formal dresses, but there is no compulsion. Visitors to the many venerated sanctuaries and shrines are naturally expected to dress modestly. Appropriate attire is also a necessity in the Mea Shearim district of Jerusalem. In the market place there is a notice in Hebrew, Yiddish and English: 'Jewish Daughters, The Torah obligates you to dress with modesty. We do not tolerate people passing through our streets immodestly dressed—Committee for Guarding Modesty.' This is more of a warning than a request and it is a fact that women in shorts have been insulted, spat on and chased from its streets. Mea Shearim, however, is certainly not indicative of the way visitors are treated in other parts of Israel!

The basic requirement for entry to Israel is a valid passport. For British citizens resident in the UK a visa is not required for a stay not exceeding three months. Citizens of the USA, Canada, Australia and New Zealand need visas, but receive them, on entry, free of charge and without previous application. An extension of stay may be obtained at any one of the district offices of the Ministry of the Interior. Any foreign national intending to work, study or settle in Israel must obtain the appropriate permit before departure.

Israel is not a cheap country, though hotel accommodation ranges from establishments of the highest international standard to moderately priced and comfortable pensions. Around 300 establishments are recommended by the Ministry of Tourism and listed in a publication produced by the Israel Hotel Association. This specifies the size of the hotel, its rates and facilities, and whether it keeps a *kosher* table. Many *kibbutzim* run their own guest-houses and are subject to the same exacting standards of service and cleanliness as Israeli hotels. They offer complete privacy and country-style food and many arrange special evening programmes to acquaint guests with *kibbutz* life. There is no obligation to participate in any communal activity nor, of course, to work, though this can be arranged and is recommended as affording a close-up view of the unique *kibbutz* phenomenon.

Would-be travellers are strongly advised to read widely about the country before setting out. The brief bibliography on page 151 may be valuable as an initial introduction to the Israeli character and the country's problems. The *Israel Government Year Book* and the numerous pamphlets issued by the Press Division of the Government Information Services cover between them almost every aspect of Israeli life and are invaluable to both student and interested layman. A varied body of literature can also be obtained from the offices of the Jewish National Fund.

An ideal way of seeing Israel quickly and comfortably is to take advantage of the excellent organised tours run by a number of licensed operators. Itineraries and prices are worked out in consultation with the Ministry of Tourism to ensure that participants see as much as possible. Tours are of half-day, full-day and two- or three-day duration, sometimes combining air travel with road transport. All organised tours are accompanied by experienced government-licensed guides who are multi-lingual.

On a more intimate level the Tourist Information Office has set up a plan whereby visitors can meet an Israeli family with interests similar to their own and be entertained to tea or coffee. Lists of local families who speak English or other languages are obtainable from all tourist offices.

For the visiting motorist many varied points of interest are located throughout the length and breadth of the country, virtually all of them easily accessible by car. An international driving licence is recognised and preferred, although a valid national driving licence printed in English and French is also acceptable. Driving is on the right and road signs in Hebrew and Arabic are invariably repeated in English. All main roads, even in the south, are surfaced and well engineered; only a few desert tracks and approach roads to nature reserves remain in poor condition. Driving in the cities can be hair-raising, and hand-signals are generally uninstructive.

There is a wide range of high-class goods which make attractive, if expensive, souvenirs of a visit—antiques, diamonds, embroideries, books, ceramics, glassware, paintings and jewellery. All shops recommended by the Ministry of Tourism carry its emblem: the two biblical 'spies' carrying a large bunch of grapes. Many establishments offer a 15-per-cent reduction if paid with foreign currency or traveller's cheques; some duty-free goods delivered to the port or airport qualify for a 30-per-cent reduction. Ben-Gurion airport offers a wide selection of duty-free goods, which have to be paid for in foreign currency. In Arab quarters, bargaining is still a tradition and the outdoor markets are filled with good buys. The first price stated usually leaves a very large margin for bargaining.

The days are gone when the Israeli haughtily refused tips. The tourists themselves have helped to foster the system, yet the outstretched palm is less in evidence than in many countries.

Cafés, restaurants and hotels are required by law to add service charges to bills and no further gratuities are necessary, except perhaps for special services. Taxi drivers expect tips only when they have carried luggage and acted as guides. Railway porters are entitled to a fixed charge of around IL1 per bag and hairdressers expect gratuities of about 10 per cent of the total bill. Cinema and theatre ushers are not tipped.

Finally, the visitor should perhaps be warned that the Israelis (excluding the Arab populations) may seem, at first, rather abrupt or even rude. Israelis are among the least subservient peoples of the world and are often not aware of the forms of ritual politeness. On the other hand they are informal, straightforward and willing to go out of their way to help the visitor once the initial overture is made. Unfortunately, this willingness to help does not necessarily mean that the visitor is being correctly advised or directed, for the Israeli is also reluctant to say, 'I don't know.' Policemen are generally more reliable about giving directions, but even they will readily consult city guides. Perhaps it should be borne in mind that the nickname for the Israeli-born is *Sabra* (Prickly Pear); it is a common dictum that he is similar to this fruit—behind a certain bluntness of manner there is a soft and tender heart.

Bibliography

Badi, J. *Religion in Israel Today: The Relationships between State and Religion* (New York, 1959)
  Fundamental Laws of the State of Israel (New York, 1961)
Baker, H. E. *The Legal System of Israel* (1961)
Bein, A. *The Return to the Soil: A History of Jewish Settlement in Israel* (Jerusalem, 1952)
Ben-Gurion, D. *Israel: Years of Challenges* (London and New York, 1964)
Bernmant, C. *Israel* (1967)
Cattan, H. *Palestine, the Arabs and Israel* (1969)
Comay, J. *Introducing Israel* (1969)
Dodds, C. H. and Sales, M. *Israel and the Arab World* (1970)
Eisenstadt, S. N. *Israeli Society* (London and New York, 1969)
Elon, A. *The Israelis* (London and New York, 1971)
Elston, D. R. *Israel: The Making of a Nation* (1963)
Friedmann, G. *The End of the Jewish People?* (1967)
Karmon, Y. *Israel: A Regional Geography* (London and New York, 1971)
Mikes, G. *The Prophet Motive: Israel Today and Tomorrow* (1969)
Prittie, T. *Israel, Miracle in the Desert* (London and New York, 1967)
Weingrod, A. *Israel, Group Relations in a New Society* (1965)

GUIDE BOOKS

Fodor, E. *Israel* (London and New York, 1973)
Levi, A. *Bazak Israel Guide* (Tel Aviv and New York, 1973)
Vilnay, Z. *The Guide to Israel* (Jerusalem and New York, 1973)

Acknowledgements

THE task of writing this book has been made very much easier by the kindness and co-operation I have received from a number of individuals and organisations both in Britain and Israel. In particular I would like to thank the staffs of the Division of Information, Ministry of Foreign Affairs, Jerusalem; the Israel Government Tourist Office, London, and the Jewish National Fund, London. All three organisations supplied me with up-to-date information on all aspects of the country and if there are imperfections in the previous pages these are the results of my own misinterpretation of the facts.

On the practical side I wish to extend my thanks for the help received from the secretarial, cartographic and photographic staffs of the Department of Geography, University of Strathclyde, Glasgow. I am especially indebted to Mrs J. C. Simpson who typed the main body of the manuscript and whose interest in its contents was a source of encouragement to me.

Finally, I would like to express my sincere thanks to Mr M. M. Johnstone for his technical advice during the preparation of this book and for his expertise in correcting manuscript and page proofs.

Index

Accommodation, 148
Adult education, 125-6
Agricultural research, 130
Agricultural schools, 121
Aircraft industry, 90
Air transport, 106-109
Alcohol, 75, 131
Aliyah, 8-14, 50
Amidar, Government Housing
    Organisation, 62
Animals, wild, 24, 134
Arabs, 8-9, 11, 14, 40, 70, 79,
    122-3
Archaeology, 2, 134, 135
Arkia Airlines, 108-9
Artists, 143-4
Ashdod, 3, 33, 87, 111-2
Ashkelon, 33, 112
Ashkenazim, 28-9, 145
Atomic energy, 88
Authors, 144-6

Balfour declaration, 11-2
Ballet, 142
Bedouin, 30, 33, 52, 60, 123
Beersheba, 21, 30, 52, 94, 129
Ben-Gurion airport, 64, 107-8,
    149
Betting, 132
Bible study, 135-6
Biblical institutes, 135-6

Biblical Patriarchs, 1-3
British mandate, 11-15, 85, 100,
    116
Broadcasting, 136-7
Buses, 104

Cabinet, 45
Cafes, 131-2, 150
Chanacuh, 133
Chemicals, 89-90
Child welfare, 66, 69-70
Choirs, 142
Christianity, 6, 31, 36, 133
Cinema, 137-8, 150
Circassians, 31
Citrus marketing board, 83
Civil service, 53-4
Climate, 23-4, 138, 147
Coastal plain, 22-3
Collective settlements, 9, 41-2,
    143
Communications, 12, 99-113
Composers, 141
Conductors, 141
Conservation, 82
Constitution, 44-5
Contour ploughing, 82
Cooperatives, 97
Courts, 51-2
Crafts, 143-4
Crops, 83-4

153

Crusades, 7, 100
Currency, 59

Defence, 57-8
Defence levy, 87
Diamonds, 90-1
Diet, 70-5
Dietary laws, 72-3
Domestic appliances, 65
Drama, 140
Dress, 147
Drink, 75, 131
Driving conditions, 149
Druze, 25, 52, 133

Eastern churches, 37
Economic growth, 76-7
Education, 114-30, 134, 135
Eilat, 87, 112-3
El Al, 106-8
Electoral system, 46, 52
El Fatah, 17
Energy, 87-8
Entertainments, 131-2, 143
Examinations, 118, 121-2
Ezra and Nehemia, operation, 26

Faizal-Weizman Agreement, 12
Fedayin, 16, 17
Festivals, 3, 132-3
Film industry, 138
Fisheries, 86
Folksongs, 142
Food, 70-5
Forestry, 84, 85-6
Fur industry, 85

Gadna Organisation, 58, 142
Galilee, 19-21, 80-4
Gaza Strip, 16, 17, 23
Geographical position, 2, 77, 99, 106
Golan Heights, 17, 19, 109

Haganah, 15
Haifa, 36-40, 104, 109, 110-1, 128, 138, 140, 141, 142
Health service, 67-9
Hebrew, 28, 29-30, 115-6, 119, 123, 125-6, 140, 144-5
Hebrew Language Council, 30
Hebrew Theatre, 139
Hippy, 120
Histadrut, 50, 96-7, 116, 139
Holidays, 132-3
Holy Places, ix, xi, 7, 31, 94, 147
Hospitals, 66, 68-9
Housing, 60-5

Immigration, 8-14, 25-7, 61-5, 77-8, 137, 138
Independence Day, 133, 137
Industry, 88-93, 111
Irrigation, 80-2
Islam, 7; see also Moslems and Arabs
Israel Defence Forces, 57-8, 119, 125, 126, 142
Israel film centre, 138

Jaffa, 10, 34, 100, 105, 131, 143; see also Tel Aviv
Jerusalem, 18, 23, 35-6, 131, 140, 142, 143
Jewish Agency, 27, 50, 54, 79, 115, 138
Jewish National Fund, 9, 50-1, 138, 148
Jezreel Valley, 20-1, 79
Jordan Valley, 21-2
Judaea, 16, 19, 21
Justice, 51-2

Karaites, 29
Kibbutzim, 41, 247, 79, 116, 124-125, 138, 139, 141, 142, 148

Kinneret, Lake, 20, 21, 23, 79, 80, 134
Kiryat Gat, 33
Kissinger peace talks, 18
Knesset, 44, 45
Kosher, 72-5
Kupat holim, 69

Labour, 94-7
Land development, 51, 79-80
Languages, 29-30
Law, 51-2
Legal system, 51-2
Libraries, 134, 135
Literature, 144-6
Livestock, 84-8
Local government, 12, 52

Maabaroth, 61
Maccabean Revolt, 5, 133
McMahon documents, 11
Magic Carpet' operation, 26, 107
Mardi Gras, 133
Matriculation, 121, 125
Medecine, 68-9, 128
Menorah, 133
Mineral resources, 87-8
Moshavim, 41-2, 79
Moslems, 30-1, 133
Multi-trend system, 116-7
Music, 140-2

Nahal, 58
National Characteristics, 150
National institutions, 49-51
National insurance, 65-6
National parks, 133
National service, 58, 121, 126
National Water Project, 17, 80
Nature reserves, 134
Navy, 58

Negev, 21, 80, 87, 100, 103, 106, 123
New Horizons movement, 143
Newspapers, 136
New towns, 33, 121, 138, 141
Nutrition, 70-1

Oil, 88-9, 110-1, 112
Old-age pensions, 66
Old Testament, 2-5
Opera, 142
Orchestras, 141-2
Orthodoxy, 9, 122, 129, 133, 137
Ottomans, 7, 8-10, 11f, 105

Palestine Liberation Organisation, 17
Partition plans, 12-15, 101
Passover Festival, 3, 133
Peel Commission, 14
Pilgrims, 94, 100
Pioneering organisations, 134
Playwrights, 140
Poets, 144-6
Police force, 54-7, 103, 150
Political situation, ix, xi, 43, 47-9
Population, 25-9, 30-1
Ports, 12, 110-13
Poultry, 85
President, 44
Press, 136
Primary schools, 118-20
Prisons, 57
Proclamation of Independence, 15, 44
Public transport, 103-5
Publishing, 135

Rabbinate, 27-8, 48, 52
Radio, 136-7
Railways, 105-6, 110-11

156 *Index*

Rambling, 134
Reading, 135
Refugees, 14, 16, 141
Religion, 2, 3, 5, 29-31, 132-3
Reparation payments, 77, 109
Research institutes, 129
Roads, 99-105
Road safety, 103
Romans, 1, 100
Rosh Hoshanah festival, 132
Rural settlement, 33, 40-1
Russian revolution, 9, 145

Sabbath, 104, 132
Sabra, 26, 145, 154
Samaria, 16, 121
Samaritans, 29
Schools, 115-22, 137, 141, 142
Scout federation, 134
Sephardim, 27-8, 145
Sheruts, 104-5
Shipping, 109-10
Simkhat Torah, 132-3
Sinai Campaign, 17, 112
Six Day War, 17-8, 70, 76, 94, 104, 109
Slums, 35, 62, 63
Social welfare, 67
Souvenirs, 149
Sport, 134
Standard of living, 60, 64, 131
State Comptroller, 53-4
Succoth, Feast of Tabernacles, 132

Taxation, 97-8, 131
Taxis, 104-5, 150
Teachers, 118-9, 123, 124, 126
Tel Aviv, 10, 22-3, 34-5, 103-4, 129, 131, 133, 136, 138, 139, 141, 143
Television, 136-7, 138
Textiles, 89

Theatre, 139-40
Tipping, 140
Torah, 5, 29, 132-3, 147
Tourism, 93, 104, 112, 109, 144, 148-9
Trade, 99, 107
Trade unions, 15, 95-7
Traffic, 103-5
Transjordan, 12, 14

'Uganda offer', 8
Ulpan, 125-6
Unemployment, 76
United Nations Special Committee on Palestine, 14
Universities, 126-9, 140, 141
Urbanisation, 32-4

Wages, 66, 95, 97-8
Walking, 134
War of Independence, 15-6, 138
Welfare state, 60, 69
Woodhead Commission, 14
Working conditions, 60, 94, 131
World War 1, 9, 10-2, 105
World War 2, 14, 77, 101, 145, 146
Writers, 144-6

Vegetation, 24, 95-6, 131
Visas, 148
Vocational schools, 121-2

Yishuv, 7
Yom Kippur, Feast of Atonement, 132
Yom Kippur War, 18, 76
Youth movements, 134

Zionism, 1, 7-15, 49, 77-8
Zionist Congress, 8, 49
Zionist Organisation, 49-50, 115, 134